THE NATURE OF REPRESENTATION

RICHARD BERNHEIMER

THE NATURE OF

REPRESENTATION

A Phenomenological Inquiry

Edited by H. W. JANSON

NEW YORK UNIVERSITY PRESS, NEW YORK

CONTENTS

v

CONTENTS

INTRODUCTION

ART HISTORIANS have long been aware that aesthetic theory, whether Plato's or Sir Herbert Read's, is to be taken at face value only if viewed as a commentary on the artistic practice of its own time and place. They have been less eager to acknowledge that their own labors—the problems they choose to investigate as well as the conceptual framework within which they see these problems—may be similarly conditioned, though perhaps in more subtle ways, by contemporary artistic events. Yet the growth of the history of art as a scholarly discipline since the days of Winckelmann cannot be fully understood unless we recognize this relationship. Thus the emergence, at the end of the last century, of Postimpressionism, with its emphasis on formal and expressive qualities at the expense of representational accuracy, had a counterpart in the art historian's new approach to the evolution of styles as an autonomous *vie des formes* and the consequent rediscovery of periods hitherto neglected as barbarous or decadent, such as Late Antiquity, the Early Middle Ages, and sixteenth-century Mannerism. Similarly, the Dadaist-Surrealist movement of the years between the two world wars, rejecting formal order and self-imposed discipline in favor of visual shock effects, a faith in spontaneity, and the exploitation of irrational impulses, helped to stimulate a greater concern among art histo-

rians with symbolism and fantasy and with the intimate
psychological aspects of artistic creation.

Since then, we have witnessed the ascendancy of a
still more radical development, variously termed Abstract Expressionism, Action Painting, or *tachisme*.
Whatever our ultimate assessment of its significance—
and the time is hardly ripe yet for such a task—we must
credit it with one notable effect: it has given us a new
perspective on the avant-garde of yesterday. Picasso,
Kandinsky, Mondrian, Klee, Miró, Ernst suddenly look
like old masters in comparison, and we realize far more
clearly than before that they are still linked to traditional values which the Action Painters seem determined
to reject. Perhaps this impression is somewhat deceptive; to future eyes, the Abstract Expressionists and
their kin will probably appear less antitraditional than
they do at present. Be that as it may, they resist analysis
in terms of the critical vocabulary developed for their
predecessors. They have thus had an important catalytic
effect in making us aware of the need to re-examine our
conceptual tools. As Dr. Bernheimer acknowledges in
the opening sentences of this book, his inquiry into the
nature of representation is a symptom of our time. We
can go further and assert that his subject is the central
problem posed by the state of painting and sculpture
today.

From the vantage point of the mid-twentieth century,
the founding fathers of abstract art a generation ago
seem "postrepresentational" rather than truly nonrepresentational; their works, whether geometric or bio-
morphic, may be nonobjective in the sense of not depicting recognizable objects, but they nevertheless refer,
however obliquely, to a reality separate from that of
the work of art itself. They still create an illusion, an

image of some kind, and to that extent retain representational significance. Action Painting, on the other hand, especially when produced by pouring, dripping, and spattering, has lost every trace of this significance. (The novel technique may indeed have been chosen for the very purpose of preventing any inadvertent representational configurations such as the beholder might be tempted to read into the marks of a brush.) The only reality to which it refers is the act of picturemaking itself. But does the picture *represent* this act? Should we not rather say that it simply records it? The term conjures up memories of photographic plates recording the tracks of atomic particles in cloud chambers—not an unsuitable simile, perhaps, since it conveys something of the explosive discharge of energy so characteristic of Action Painting. Yet in calling the Action Painter's shapes "tracks," and the picture itself a "record," we imply that such canvases are mere by-products or echoes of the action that brought them forth, as if the artist had been indulging in a kind of exercise that involved the manipulation of paint only incidentally. This is treacherous ground, for who can be sure that the Action Painter at work is less fully intent on picturemaking than the artists of old? The same objection prevents us from speaking of his configurations as "gestures" instead of "tracks." Nor do we come any closer to their true meaning if we term them "signs" or "symbols," as the semanticists would have us do. What we need, clearly, is a framework theory, a "semantics of the visual arts" that will allot to each of these terms its proper significance and thus (in Dr. Bernheimer's words) "provide a common ground upon which the proponents of antagonistic points of view in aesthetics may take their stand."

That such a theory should be based on the concept

of representation can be argued on historical, philosophical, and psychological grounds. The mere fact that until very recently the representational function of art was simply taken for granted and hence remained unanalyzed bespeaks the fundamental importance of the phenomenon explored in these pages. Significantly enough, Dr. Bernheimer is not the only scholar to have recognized the need for a theory of representation. Several others have been preoccupied with the same problem during the past decade, although in less comprehensive and systematic fashion. The most penetrating among these is E. H. Gombrich, who dealt with the subject in a famous essay of 1951, "Meditations on a Hobby Horse, or the Roots of Artistic Form," and at greater length in his A. W. Mellon Lectures of 1956 at the National Gallery of Art in Washington, published in 1960 under the title, *Art and Illusion: A Study in the Psychology of Pictorial Representation*. Despite differences of method and emphasis, *Art and Illusion* shares many insights with *The Nature of Representation*. The two books complement and illuminate each other. Between them they have laid the groundwork for a far-reaching reinterpretation of the genesis of art and its ever-changing role in the human community.

Richard Bernheimer's concern with the analysis of representation goes back as far as 1939. In that year, at a symposium on art at Bryn Mawr College, he presented two papers of seminal importance (subsequently published in *Bryn Mawr Notes and Monographs*, IX, 1940), "In Defense of Representation" and "Concerning Symbols." These early fruits of his inquiry, largely overlooked in the turmoil of the war years, became the point of departure for the present book. (The somewhat polemical title of the first paper must not be misunderstood; it is directed not against modern art but against those of its partisans who dismiss all representation as extraneous to the *raison d'être* of art.) The manuscript grew but slowly, its progress impeded both by the inherent difficulty of the subject and by the author's preoccupation with problems of a more strictly historic kind. By 1958, the year of his untimely death, he had nevertheless completed the project, except for a final chapter or summary that remained unwritten. When his executor entrusted me with the task of preparing the manuscript for publication, I soon realized that neither I nor any of Richard Bernheimer's other friends and colleagues could attempt to supply such a summing up without grave risk of distorting his intent. I have therefore confined my editorship to minor revisions of the text for the sake of clarity and readability, such as the author himself might have made in the process of seeing the book through publication.

H. W. J.

THE NATURE OF REPRESENTATION

1 The Problem

The fact that the present essay came to be written can be regarded as a minor symptom of our time. To investigate the function and inner structure of artistic representation, instead of concentrating upon the manner in which it is to be achieved, would not have occurred to thinkers of the past who had every reason for taking that function for granted. For them, painting and sculpture were by nature representational arts, whose task was the imitation of phenomena from the outer world. All that the artist could do was to take a stand toward these phenomena, to accept them as they were, to improve them by idealization, or to transcend them by recourse to those eternal Platonic ideas from which their shapes were supposed to have been derived. It was taken for granted that the artist was to treat a subject familiar to the members of his community and that he was to interpret and elucidate it, limiting what he had to say to a new insight into matters known to all.

This comfortably circumscribed artistic world, in which everybody could find his bearings, was blasted wide open by the advent, in this century, of the various forms of abstract and nonobjective art. It was discovered that beyond the range of recognizable and familiar subject matter lay another range of vaster proportions, but of baffling indeterminacy, in which the rules hitherto taken for granted did not seem to hold. Representation, instead of being the accepted method of art, became its casual by-product, and thus ceased to offer insight into the world of experience, of which, at best, it contained only reminiscences.

But as the interest in the outright rendering of things was purged from the artist's consciousness, representation re-established itself in his work under a new guise. He found that only a rather puritanical limitation to elementary geometric forms assured to his creation its abstract character. If he let his imagination play beyond the narrow demarkations which his aesthetic creed imposed upon his art, then the habit of thinking in terms of the known would reassert itself: shapes derived from the world of sense experience would re-enter into his creation, but this time not as renditions of objects reliably placed in space and time, but as subjective images. Their choice would depend not upon a conscious determination of subject matter preceding the creation of the work of art, but upon inner events released by the creative process itself over which the artist would not want to exert more than a partial control. Surrealism and abstract art are thus related not only historically, but also genetically at their psychological roots. When, early in this century, artists began to break up the living forms of things into geometric shapes increasingly removed from reality, they opened the path for another trend, a movement toward subjective imagery.

The retreat from likeness which has thus marked the art of our time poses the problem of representation in several new ways: it compels us to inquire into the limitations of the abstract and to find out at what point, and because of what energies inherent in the configuration itself, a design acquires representational capacity; it compels us to investigate the social function of representation, which in the past served the communication between all well-informed members of a cultural community, while today, in its surrealist form, it reflects the private world of the artist only and must be put across through the rather fortuitous stimulation of recondite psychic processes. Finally, and most important, the existence of abstract and surrealist art suggests that there may be several levels of visual representation that cannot be equated with each other, any more than we can equate the incongruous imagery of a dream with the coherence and lucidity of normal waking experience. The surrealists themselves underline the special character of what they have to offer by claiming for their output the dignity of a symbolic revelation: a dignity that can be accorded to it only if we accept their claim that they have succeeded in making psychic processes visible to the outer eye and that these are, as Freud insists, essentially symbolic. This claim, like all scientific pronouncements meant to bolster artistic tendencies, must be treated with reserve.

Still, no matter what we may think of the surrealist use of psychoanalytic thought, the introduction of the word "symbol" into the discussion is in itself of considerable importance for any modern theory of representation. The word is admittedly one of the most protean in the language. But however it is defined—and we shall have to dwell upon its many ambiguities—it clearly suggests a mode of functioning different from that which we attribute to simple likenesses. Transcending the realm of mere visual similarities, all symbols tend to bring us into contact with realities otherwise partly or totally inaccessible. It matters little in this connection whether this contact be attained with or without man's conscious direction, whether it be communal or private, religious or the mere uncontrolled release of perhaps unworthy strivings and impulses. It would seem likely, even without detailed analysis, that a symbol—any symbol—functions by virtue of an inner process more recondite and more penetrating than that which governs our understanding of simple likenesses. Theories of representation which overlook this disparity have little chance of reflecting more than a mere fraction of the truth.

A cursory examination of contemporary art thus compels us to realize that representation is not the simple function it may appear to be to the casual and nonreflective observer; and that it possesses a complex structure of its own, of which any theoretical account will have to take cognizance. It is possible and even necessary to extend this insight to the intellectual environment in which contemporary art grew and flourishes, for a comprehensive theory of representation should be able to provide a common ground upon which the proponents of antagonistic points of view in aesthetics may take their stand.

We have among us the theoreticians of abstract art and the abstract theoreticians of art, who condemn all representational content as irrelevant and insist that aesthetic effect is based upon the unadulterated values of line and color. Their attitude is often so infuriatingly rigid and dogmatic that the very manner in which they state their creed makes one wonder what may have been the innate functions and merits of that older representational art which they dismiss so peremptorily. An almost equally rigorous countermovement in criticism concerns itself mainly with the analysis of representational content, striving to bring to light the long-forgotten meanings—allegorical, emblematic, and symbolic—with which many works of traditional art used to delight the beholder trained to appreciate their intellectual subtleties. Although not much sympathy is lost between these two camps, the very fact that they are able to approach the same subject in mutually exclusive ways suggests that both are aware only of aspects of a more comprehensive truth transcending their particular points of view. There is no more than fleeting contact between either school of criticism and that growing body of psychological and religious thought which is centered around the concept of the symbol, although, as we saw, that concept is eminently applicable to certain artistic phenomena. If we add to this the fact that the psychologists concerned with the problem of symbolism are in their turn divided into schools, each with its more or less parochial creed, then we become aware of the crying need for a common language embodied in a common theory. Such a theory would have to assign to each school of thought its proper place within a vaster structure, and thus would help to create the condition without which no valid general thought can be conceived. It would help to combat the stultifying factionalism and the narrowing of interest upon specialized methods and subjects which has done so much to diminish the authority of the humanities.

The present essay on representation is meant as a contribution toward such a theory.

II *Theories of Representation*

Of the existing theories of artistic representation, by far the oldest and most widespread maintains that it is the function of art to imitate, to imitate in a literal and relentless fashion, allowing no space for a personal contribution by the artist, and confining the work of art to the role of an indistinguishable duplicate of its model. The purpose of such transcription, if this theory be taken seriously, is the deception of the unwary, who are induced to take the artifact for the natural object from which it has been copied. Zeuxis, according to Pliny, painted a bunch of grapes so well that the birds swooped down upon them; Parrhasius, undaunted, painted a curtain, which an artist friend and competitor tried to lift in order to inspect the picture he believed underneath.

The astonishing thing about these stories and many others like them—the aspect that requires explanation—

7

is not so much that they were invented and told, but that the telling was supposed to redound to the artist's praise, for we are not inclined to accept visual deception as an artistic accomplishment. On the contrary, any sound theory must hold that we find ourselves beyond the pale of art if there can be a moment's doubt whether the work of painting or sculpture before us belongs to the world of artistic contemplation or to that of our practical affairs.

One may attempt therefore to give some of the credit which we must withhold from the theory of deception to its toned-down version which demands from the artist that he at least approximate nature as closely as possible, even though complete illusion is not expected of him. It is the view, widespread among unsophisticated laymen of all times, that sees the merit of art in the painstakingly faithful reproduction of the lively glance, the creased surface, and other visual phenomena. But this theory, like the other, runs into simple and fundamental objections. For if it is the task of art to reproduce nature, without choice or preference, then how can the artist, taking his start from indiscriminate observation, ever arrive at the creation of the beautiful? To explain this seeming miracle, it is necessary to resort to subsidiary theories, of which there have been a small number in the course of time. Most of them suffer from the fatal weakness of presupposing that which they set out to explain.

It will not do, for instance—to take a particularly primitive example—to say as Pliny does, in connection with Apelles, that the artist assured the beauty of his product by choosing a beautiful model, or—what is worse—several of them, whose finest parts he combined. For in order to make his selection, the artist must know in advance what is beautiful, and on the basis of his activity as a copyist, he is not capable of that. The same objection holds of any theory obliging the artist to correct reality by the application of a system of proportions, for nothing in his reproductive work enables him to recognize the mathematical code in which the secret of the beautiful is supposed to be enshrined.

The only manner in which the difficulties involved in a theory of indiscriminate imitation can be overcome at all is by the frank recognition that what the artist copies is not the humdrum visual object, beautiful as it may be, but a corrected version of it which exists either in his own mind or in a superworldly realm of Platonic ideas to which he may have the privilege of access. Whoever affirms this theory will have to ask himself, however, whether he is ready also to assent to its far-reaching psychological and metaphysical implications which, although largely unquestioned in the centuries of Neoplatonic dominance, are difficult to accept today.

There is another and even more fundamental objection against the theory of indiscriminate imitation, which arises not from the theory's inability to fulfill the demands of beauty but from its failure to attribute to art any convincing purpose. What good, one might ask, could possibly come of activities such as painting and sculpture, which demand tremendous exertions from their practitioners, if the result be a mere counterfeit of reality, without the inner structure, the mobility and spontaneity of which natural things can boast? Or, to speak with Plato, who was the first to feel and formulate the absurdity of a purely imitative art: what could be the point in creating visual duplicates of things which themselves, if we accept Plato's theory of ideas, are secondary and derivative, so that the artist's creation is in fact twice removed from reality? Art, thus regarded, becomes *"simia naturae,"* a mere ape of nature; it was thus branded for centuries in the conviction that it was a self-defeating activity, devoted to the impossible task of reproducing that which was forever escaping it.

We might add, viewing the matter in psychological terms, that imitation as such is justified only if it is part of a playful activity resulting from an exuberance of spirit or from the need of the young to learn the ways of the adult world. Unless it is organized into play-acting, which rests on "aping" as a creative principle, imitation tends to become the mark of weak personalities doomed by their lack of character to forever reflecting the manners of the strong. The imitative activity imputed to the painter and sculptor, requiring as it does long and patient work by an adult, serves neither of these purposes; it does not prepare the artist for life, nor does it enhance his enjoyment of it. It falls short, therefore, of those legitimate functions which a sound psychological theory would attribute to imitative behavior. Unless there is in art a deeper purpose than the mere duplication of reality, it might just as well be abandoned.

Unsatisfactory, then, as the theory of indiscriminate imitation is, its very formulation and the frequency with which it is applied are due to deep-seated needs and habits, individual and collective. It can be shown that the demand for a painstaking imitation of nature is itself descended historically and genetically from an older attitude which asked for visual objects capable of replacing their prototypes and of being identified with them: objects rendered so thoroughly alive by their relation to what they represent that they take on the function of their originals. Thus, before there was a demand for likenesses capable of deceiving the beholder, there was a demand for images which could dispense with such trickery because they simply were that which the others only pretended to be. And both these attitudes preceded the formulation of an imitative aesthetic.

At the root, then, of the theory of indiscriminate imitation is the magical belief in the identity of the likeness with what it represents : a belief which naturally results in attributing to the likeness powers and capabilities which in a rationally ordered world would belong only to primary phenomena. It is this belief which engendered such ancient Greek myths as that of Daidalos the sculptor whose products were able to move or even to speak so that they had to be fettered to prevent them from running away; or such Christian legends as that in Pseudo-Matthew about the idols in an Egyptian temple which broke in two when the entry of the Christ child made them realize that the time of their rule had passed; or again the stories connected with some miraculous Madonnas that these images had traversed the sea of their own free will from Byzantium to their present station in the Western world. The very fact that such Madonnas are regarded as miraculous indicates that they are believed to share the powers of the Queen of Heaven, whose likeness they are supposed to transmit; in fact that these powers are particularized and channeled through them. In a special and complex sense miraculous Madonnas are the living presence of the Queen of Heaven herself.

It must be added that there is little direct relation between what we call the style of a picture or statue and the aliveness and reality which popular superstition may attribute to it. On the contrary, legends about the strange activities of idols may arise in primitive periods of art or they may attach themselves to objects of a simple and undeveloped kind, whose style is at variance with current, more advanced practices. The less a work of art fulfills the demands of a realistic aesthetic, the more it is prone to be credited with those miraculous activities which seem to be belied by its appearance. Even praise for deceptiveness, or at least for thoroughgoing fidelity to nature, may be accorded (although it does not have to be) to works of art which by any standard of realism would be regarded as well within the limits of a discreetly traditional procedure. Such praise often betrays a pattern of thought which precedes the experience of the individual work of art, and thus needs to be adjusted to it only superficially. The nonconformity between the theory of imitation and the works of art to which it is said to apply will occupy us later.

It was Aristotle's merit to have removed the most glaring inconsistencies in the theory of representation by claiming that what imitation means to render is not the individual object with its inevitable departure from the norm, but its class or species: a thesis which reflects the philosopher's acquaintance with Greek art and with its perennial allegiance to the embodied generic type. Many of the difficulties inherent in the older theory were thus swept away with one stroke; for clearly, if what the artist created was the visible embodiment of the type, then his work ceased to be a mere duplicate of natural phenomena, none of which ever succeeded in exhibiting the ideal form of its species uncontaminated. It was the artist's privilege, in fact, to accomplish nature's aim where nature herself failed, incapable as she was of overcoming the resistance of matter to the unfolding of its potentialities.

Once Aristotle's opinion was adopted, art could no

longer be viewed as a pointless or self-defeating activity, for it served the high intellectual purpose of revealing the generic norm, which, without its assistance, would be hidden under the wild growth of imperfect individual specimens. Moreover, an art which shows what things should be rather than what they are could not but exert a strong educational function as well by confronting man with the image of what he could become if he succeeded in realizing his own dormant capabilities. Since art, in this view, was designed to affect human life as an aesthetic and ethical paragon, it overcame all arguments against it which derived their strength from its imputed social uselessness. Only an idealistic art was capable of this. It should be noted, therefore, that both Aristotle's theory generally and its pedagogical implication had their origin in Greek art which had at all times served the improvement of the human type. From the very start it had set out to bridge the gap between the human and the divine by the creation of perfect human specimens. What it exhibited on the temple pediments, on the market places and in the frescos in public buildings was an invitation to the beholder to strive toward an organic evolution of his powers similar to what he saw before him. Even later, when the educational purpose of Greek art had given way to the aesthetic dogmatism of classicist revivals, the ideal recommended or attained was looked upon as a paragon of human perfection made to spur man to noble accomplishments.

Effective, then, as Aristotle's theory of imitation was, its signal success should not blind us to its shortcomings. Like the theory of indiscriminate imitation it failed to provide the artist with a guide toward the beautiful (if by "beautiful" be meant the realization of the generic type), leaving it to him to find a recipe for its discovery. Nor could the few words that Aristotle devoted to the theory of representation furnish the thinker with a reliable tool for determining whether the type of which the philosopher spoke was an average, so to speak, between divergent specimens, such as the compound photograph of superimposed faces, or whether it really was the ideal which surpassed them all; a distinction important enough to mark the difference between two kinds of thought and of art.

In addition Aristotle's theory, as it was usually interpreted, bore a limitation which restricted its applicability. For assuming that he meant to refer not to the mean but to the ideal distilled from imperfect samples and specimens, then it followed that the species which the artist interpreted could hardly be any other than man himself. A Platonist might conceive of the eternal idea of such indifferent objects as, say, an apple, a chair, or a curtain; an Aristotelian, on the other hand, could apply the term "ideal" only to things capable of improvement through the selfless application of human energy and of promoting, through their betterment, man's spiritual aspirations. First and foremost among things thus defined is man himself.

We find, therefore, that an idealistic art such as the Greek must also be anthropomorphic. If we apply our findings to a period which, although aware of Aristotle's theory, produced genres of art other than those pertaining only to human excellence, we discover that it was natural and even necessary that the thinkers of the seventeenth and eighteenth centuries who endorsed Aristotle's thought should have insisted upon a gradation of artistic subjects, placing at the bottom still life and portraiture and at the summit the "historical" themes, which showed man at his noble best. Only these themes, it was believed, allowed the artist to appeal to the better nature of his public by combining the choice of a lofty subject with an equally sublime treatment of it. Once the heroic character of the artist's work was thus assured, then the supplementary theories of classicism came into play: theories which dealt with the adequacy to the subject-matter shown of gesture, facial expression, and of external paraphernalia, and thus made certain that the details of the artist's work were in accord with his central conviction. Under no circumstances could the Aristotelian theorist allow that the so-called lower genres—portraiture, landscape, and still life— be put on the same level with his own field of preference, for such democratic equalization appeared to him as an attack upon fundamental ethical tenets.

It was therefore a real revolution against a general and well-established order when progressive theorists of the eighteenth and particularly of the nineteenth century began to lay siege to the hierarchy of subject-matter by declaring that it was never the choice of a theme which determined the rank of a work of art but only the manner in which it had been approached; and that a truly revealing and penetrating treatment could glorify any subject, no matter how lowly. This new attitude reflected the then modern artistic development which favored a factual interpretation of life over idealistic pretensions, producing landscapes, genre, and still lifes of superior excellence. It seemed all the easier to take this stand, since in the beginning, at least, the abandonment of the rigid Aristotelian doctrine did not necessarily imply that the assumed superiority of art over reality had to be given up, too; the transition was eased by the curious concept of the picturesque, which permitted man to rediscover qualities derived from pictures in the real landscapes through which he passed on his travels, or in scenes of everyday life. Although the experiences thus projected into man's practical environment were not all-inclusive and ethical, as they had been under the reign of Aristotelian thought, they still served to single out for art a function as a guide and paradigm: its pedagogical task was now narrowed down to the teaching of visual charm in casual and haphazard phenomena.

Despite these harmless early manifestations, the doctrine of the equality of subjects was to have truly revolutionary consequences, for carried to its ultimate conclusions it led to the destruction of representation itself. Representation was safe only as long as the particular inherent spirit of each subject was acknowledged in its distinctiveness; it was safe only as long as the lushness of fruit, the assertion of low instinct by drunken brawlers in an inn, the rigid dignity of an officeholder, and similar values held the attention of the artist. It must be recognized, however, that while these implied or (as proponents of abstract art call them) associative values were still given their due, there could as yet be no real equality of genres. These values belong to a great hierarchy, the existence of which every human being must recognize, no matter what attitude he may take toward it and how he may want to order its components. Therefore, wherever such values are shown in art, our judgment of their place in human life is bound to modify our critical stand and the quality of our aesthetic enjoyment.

It is only when all representational types and genres are reduced to their lowest visual denominators, as they were in the later years of the nineteenth century, that representation itself is imperiled. For then a situation is created analogous to the effect of the leveling of personal characteristics in a mass society: distinctions are swept away, signs of individuality erased; and just as the universal lowering of level in a mass society may blot out what we have learned to regard as distinctively human, so in art the disappearance of essential nonvisual characteristics may sweep representation out of existence. What remains after the expulsion of "associative values" are only the patterns, shapes, and colored surfaces that all objects have in common, be they vases, the flowers they contain, the contour of a distant mountain, or a human face. Since objects thus conceived are not entitled to any preference over abstract configurations composed of the same simple elements, there is no reason henceforth why the artist should limit himself to representing objects drawn from reality. He may rather want to set sail for unknown isles in the ocean of abstraction.

Historically the first step toward abstract art was taken when it occurred to an artist to treat the human figure as if it were a pictorial motif from a still life, omitting those unique qualities which raise man above the level of inert matter or of a merely vegetative existence. This initial equalization of subjects through the lowering of the human status was accomplished in the figure studies by Corot and Manet. The Impressionists followed suit through their radical exclusion from painting of all nonvisual values, leaving to their heirs the task of crystallizing into colored patterns the pictorial material which they had been the first to isolate.

It goes without saying that a period which saw the destruction of "Aristotelian"—i.e., Academic—art could not produce any new idealistic theory of representation;

nor could real originality be expected from the natural-
istic theories of the nineteenth century, which were
merely the aesthetic doctrine of indiscriminate imitation
raised to the status of an artistic creed. The modern
age has nevertheless brought forth its own distinctive
doctrine of representation, although it had to abandon
any attempt to derive the origin of representation from
such positive impulses as the desire to imitate or to
establish a standard of perfection. Beset by the loss of
values which sustained the generations of the past and
by the demons which dwell in the ensuing emptiness, our
age conceives of representation as the result not of an
abundance of life, but of a haunting fear. Representation, according to this theory, is a magical defense
against the inexorable passage of time and the menace
of demoniacal powers. To these vague and shapeless
threats it opposes its own permanence and the clear-cut
definition of its design, reflecting man's desire for order,
measure, and stability.

Specifically, in its apotropaic form, representation
confounds the demon by throwing back at him his own
concentrated image, which he cannot tolerate. Speaking
more generally, representation is an assertion of man's
ability to vanquish the powers that beset him, either by
erecting monuments to his own immortality or by making the images of demons available for sorcery. In either
case representation serves as the expression of man's
power over the unknown and thus increases the area of
his security. It helps him to acquire confidence in his
own continuity and provides him with the means through
which this continuity can be assured.

The theory thus furnishes an insight into an early
period in the history of representation, a period not
yet sufficiently reflective to speculate about its own

activities; it brings us closer to the origins of a fundamental human function than do the other explanations; and because it deals with basic human impulses, it has the additional advantage that it can marshal for its support an enormous material, ethnological and archeological, which shows that at the beginning of all civilizations and throughout the whole extent of those which we label primitive, representation does largely serve the purposes outlined above. Wherever magic designs provide the environment for a cult, wherever a demon is rendered in his original frightfulness or where his face is used to decorate man's tools, there art retains some of its defensive purpose. Its contribution to human immortality is recorded in works of art such as the sculptures and paintings in the Egyptian tombs, which provide man with the means of living in effigy beyond the time of his physical death.

The magical explanation of representation thus provides a more plausible motive for its origin than do the theories that postulate an always hypothetical desire to imitate. The new theory holds that imitation is merely a tool in the hands of men intent upon more vital ends. Instead of conceiving of representation as the effect of an alleged imitative instinct hardly basic and comprehensive enough to explain the ubiquity of art, the modern theory regards it as an important implement in the general human effort to adjust to the world at large. According to this view, representation derives from the same profound needs that caused the rise of the nonrepresentational arts. Architecture in particular, with which sculpture and painting are often so intimately linked, can be understood as a defense against the immensity of space and the relentless flux of time, undertaken through the reduction of the limitless to a system of measurable and rhythmically determined parts. It, too, like the representational arts, seems to be born out of primordial fear.

The merit of the magical theory of representation is thus demonstrable. It would be dangerous, however, to let oneself be enticed by its success into looking upon it as a panacea. Like all modern attempts at explaining advanced human activities in terms of their primitive origins, the theory breaks down when universalized. It cannot account for the qualitative differences which appear in the course of the history of art. It is unable, therefore, to do justice to an art which, like the Greek, succeeded in emancipating itself from the dominance of magical purposes. Nor is it capable of advancing our comprehension of great masters of the more recent past, who have striven to offer an insight into the world surrounding us, and thus have enriched our inner life instead of merely protecting us. Whenever art attempts to penetrate into the nature of its subjects instead of condensing their magical potential, it raises itself by the direction of its effort beyond the rule of the primordial drives from which it originated. If we are to keep pace with the phenomena we set out to explain, the magical theory of representation will have to be at least supplemented and perhaps replaced by ideas from other quarters.

III *Representation and Sign Function*

As we examine once more the theories we have passed in review, it becomes apparent that they are successful only as long as they deal with the purpose of representation or with its presumptive origin, while they hardly advance beyond surmise when trying to cope with the problem of its structure, an indication that our knowledge has not yet reached the stage of philosophical maturity.

A promise of closing this rather serious gap is held out by the recently constituted science of semantics, which attempts to solve the problems of human behavior and cognition by concentrating upon the instruments which the mind holds ready for its task. Representation, so the semanticists say, is only a part of man's vast armory of manipulated signs, which provide him with the means of gaining knowledge, formulating and communicating it, and thus of governing the behavior of the group. If he is not overly interested in phenomenological niceties, the semanticist may even imply that between signification and representation as defined by him there exists no really meaningful distinction, so that it becomes legitimate to use both terms interchangeably.

In order to hold this view, it is necessary to simplify the problem by reducing it to the test case of language (as Cassirer has done in his *Philosophie der symbolischen Formen*). Language, as we shall see, does indeed draw its vitality from the overlapping of representational and semantic categories. It may fairly be doubted, however, whether a philosophy such as this, which takes its start from the notoriously most complex —and therefore most elastic—of all human functions, is capable also of doing justice to simpler relationships. Cassirer's method allows the assemblage of vast amounts of information under a few simple theoretical considerations and thus is supremely successful as a working hypothesis. His book remains the magnificent achievement that it is, despite serious weaknesses in its foundations, only because it deals less with real signs and things which represent than with the concrete problems of myth, language, and scientific thought, which are expressed in their terms. As a demonstration of how semantic concepts can be used to understand the various forms of human knowledge the book is unsurpassed. It makes no direct contribution, however, to the problem of artistic representation, which its author has omitted, presumably because it seemed too remote from his central linguistic and cognitive interests to engage his attention.

In contrast to Cassirer, the American scientific semanticists, foremost among whom are Charles Peirce and Bertrand Morris, refuse to be drawn into concrete linguistic problems, since they view their task as primarily analytical. Their aim is a complete and rational classification of all signs as a preamble to a later recording of the types of human knowledge. Their method compels them therefore to devote most of their attention to the ideals of neatness and conceptual clarity. So intent are they, in fact, upon descriptive precision at the expense of all other values, that they usually fail when trying to do justice to the higher, more complex human functions such as poetry, which tend to take flight when approached with the scalpel of analytical thought. Representation in all its forms they treat as a rather minor matter not important enough to deserve more than a little corner within their vast intellectual systems. As adherents to the pragmatist school of thought or to its behaviorist extreme, they demand of a semantic theory that it explain human mental activities as manipulations pointed toward immediate and tangible results, since man himself is conceived by them as a creature designed to respond to stimuli or to overcome pressures by the intelligent application of sign processes. As captives of a confining philosophical creed they find it difficult to do justice to a human function such as representation, which demands not the nimble manipulation of mental materials but a receptive attitude and the humble contemplation of that which is put before us. There is no place for contemplation or humility in an activist philosophy; and we find therefore that semanticists tend to defer to the future the analysis of a function which embarrasses them and defies their ways of thought by the slowness of its effect, by the psychological depth to which it may be able to penetrate, and by the long and continuous concentration required of the beholder if he is to avail himself of its benefits.

Nor have semanticists the means of appreciating the activity of the artist creating a representational work of art, since the artist is not at liberty, any more than the onlooker, to produce novelty through the intelligent combination of signs. His task is defined by the nature of the subject put before him and by the felt necessity to realize its values through a treatment adequate to them. Creative as his contribution is, it is not free once representation has begun to cast its spell over him.

We find in short that the promise which modern semantics seemed to hold out to us of solving the problem of artistic representation is not kept. We may go further and say that it cannot be kept, since, except for language, the identity postulated by semanticists between representation and sign processes is illusory. It may be well, therefore, to forestall later disagreement or misunderstanding by stating now, somewhat too abruptly perhaps, and as yet without explanation or proof, how we must differ from recent semantic theory. We will use the opportunity which offers itself to set down in simple and affirmative terms some of the tenets to the demonstration of which this book is dedicated.

It is proposed, then, to show that the current identification of representation with sign function is illegitimate; that while the two modes of apprehension overlap, the field of representation is wider than the area it shares with its sister function, comprising phenomena which no theory of semantics, however constituted, can ever claim for itself; that representation has an inner structure of its own, akin to but by no means identical with that possessed by various categories of signs; and finally that the function most akin to representation is not, as semanticists suppose, that of signification, but the much neglected and little known one of substitution. In order to prove such far-reaching claims, we shall have to widen the scope of our speculation beyond its original application to art, extending our interest to whatever promises to help reveal the nature of the function we seek to understand. The time spent on seemingly distant matters will not be lost: the knowledge gained will prove useful for any complete analysis of artistic phenomena, particularly as we ascend from reproductive representation to its higher symbolic phases.

What, after all, is the hallmark of what we call representation? In English and its relatives in the Romance family of languages, the word may be used in several well-defined, though closely related contexts: We speak of a picture representing its subject, a lawyer his client, a sample the species of which it is part, or again of a symbol representing the powerful but perhaps obscure realities to which it may hold the key. In each case there is, as the Latin word suggests, an element of "presence" and an element of "vicariousness" which tend to invalidate it. We find ourselves invited to examine at leisure what the object that represents, or the "representamen" as we shall call it, has to offer us, and to treat and study its message as if it were entirely its own, without reference to anything beyond it. A good picture, an attorney or a parliamentarian in action, can exert a very powerful fascination that for some time may erase all awareness of a second dimension behind their immediate visible and audible appeal. And yet, if we give representation its due, we know that its exponent stands in a relation of dependence upon another entity placed dimly in the background, an entity which, although it may never appear, is yet responsible for the representational capacity of the representamen. If a picture has no subject, an attorney no clients, a parliamentarian no voters to whom he is responsible, their representational function is void. There is, therefore, in all genuine representation a dialectic between its appearance and the content it is to convey. Because of the tensions it generates, this dialetic bestows upon representation a vitality shared by no other function.

It is this dialectic which is absent from all pure sign functions. Signs do not stand before us, as representamina do, to be examined, studied, enjoyed, weighed, and estimated. They do so only to be transcended, for signs are stimuli meant to arouse an immediate appropriate response, and thus are ready to be obliterated in our consciousness as soon as their business is done. The perfect reaction to a sign is to forget that it has occurred the moment the sequel has taken place. The perfect sign is one that subsists without individuality, character, and internal qualities, a mere empty shell of its own function. I need not insist that signs of this kind have long been in existence and that they have proved useful indeed, because their very emptiness assures their universal application. The algebraic signs and those of the logical calculus are of this order.

The difference between representation and signification is thus a fundamental and radical one. It must be conceded, however, that in ordinary experience the vacuity of signs does not make itself felt in its disheartening barrenness as much as our theoretical analysis demands, for the nature of mind forbids the total obliteration of anything that once was a content of consciousness. After a word has been spoken, or a bell has been rung, awareness of the fact lingers on, while the appropriate reaction—mental or physical—takes place. It can even be claimed that the ability to perceive both the sign and one's own response to it, though the sign may have come from one's own vocal cords, is among the distinguishing marks of human consciousness. Only as we descend below the human level do we reach a biological stage where the response to signs is automatic and unreflective, causing a state of dependence upon stimuli so complete that it excludes awareness of their presence. We must imagine, in consequence, that the world of lower animals is entirely without experienced qualities, empty and incoherent, a mere network of potential occasions for unfailingly directed reflexes.

Signs are so constituted that their mere presence before a properly trained observer is sufficient to endow them with the function they are meant to discharge. We can say, therefore, that the mere presence of smoke is a sign of fire, or that the presence of a symptom is a sign of illness, for accumulated experience has taught us to pass instantaneously from any such indication to the cause we have always found associated with it. The only delay that may take place will be due to the necessity, which sometimes arises, of discovering subordinate signs to establish that the object before us is in fact a sign. All that is required of us in dealing with such auxiliary indications will again be to find sufficient evidence of their presence, upon the detection of which the semantic process will unroll automatically.

What is true of indications of all kinds is valid also for conventional signs, including those which constitute the vocabulary of our languages, except that the instantaneous response, which in the first case was due to experience, must now be attributed to the acceptance by both speaker and listener of rules linking a complex of sounds to a so-called meaning. Once this connection has been made through learning, the listener will be able to grasp the intentions of the speaker immediately in and through the spoken word. No analysis is called for unless the speaker's choice of means has left a doubt as to what he wanted to convey. When the language used and its relation to the subject embodied in it are themselves experienced as sources of enjoyment, upon which one may want to dwell as one does upon elevated prose and still more upon poetry, then (in a sense to be analyzed later) there has been a profound penetration of the semantic material with representational values.

It can never be demanded that a single sign, be it indicative or conventional, have anything in common with the entity to which it points beyond the dynamic relation which unites the two. A sign need not resemble its referent nor does it need to belong to the same species or category, so long as experience or an established rule enables it to fulfill its task. Since it is, as we saw, an empty receptacle for its own function, it cannot make its inner characteristics available for participation in the semantic process, except as means of establishing its own identity. Its relation to its referent is therefore always, if you will, extrinsic and arbitrary.

It is possible, however—and this helps to bridge the gap between signs and representamina—to endow signs with a certain resemblance to what we mean to say, by combining them externally according to a rule. We speak then of the syntactic dimension of sign function, which is the basis for language. The manipulations and combinations thus made possible permit the speaker to compensate for the inner poverty of the signs to which he must resort, through the wealth of associations into which he may make them enter. Provided that he limit himself to a descriptive mode of speech, excluding calls, commands, and questions, he will thus be able to introduce into language a representational element, the strength of which he can regulate through the suggestiveness, detail, and intimacy of his statement.

The unique elasticity of language, its ability to extend its range from the simplest and most abstract judgment to vivacious narrative, is very largely due to this fusion of representational with semantic elements, which permits any shift of emphasis. A speaker can limit himself to elementary affirmations or negations. He can also, if he so desires and if he possesses the requisite power over words, put all the functional units of language at the service of its descriptive capacity. Which mode he prefers will depend upon whether what he has to say serves the purposes of elementary communication within the give and take of human intercourse, or whether it is to be set apart, to be told as a tale on a winter evening, to be perused as a novel, or to be studied as a scientific tract.

It must be emphasized, however, that as the representational element in language increases, there is a growing tendency to lift the unit to which it belongs out of its context, to sever its syntactic relationships, and to present it as a thing sufficient unto itself. For representation does not and need not possess syntactic properties —this is one of its better-marked characteristics. It does not require the supplementary contact and interaction with other units of its kind, through which linguistic signs overbalance their own vacuity; for the representamen is itself always stable and rich enough to attract and hold attention. What signs must accomplish through their external concatenation, representation achieves by exhibiting its inner properties. In language, therefore, syntactic and representational functions are mutually complementary. They apply to the same units of speech and of literature, except that the first is a constructive principle whose lever is the single sign seeking fulfillment through association with others, while the second is a principle of order organizing the whole, be it a paragraph, chapter, or book to which the sign is contributing.

Needless to say, the same linguistic fabric appears very differently from the two vantage points; that which to the grammarian or logician, seeing it from within, is a network strung together in application of a set of rules, is to the literary critic the presentation of a content within a form appropriate to it. Language profits from this interlocking of two principles of which one determines its mode of progression and continuity, while the other stamps the sequence of words evolved with its descriptive individuality.

When it comes to nonlinguistic forms of representation, we find that they have little tolerance for syntactic adjunctions. Lawyers and ambassadors—good and typical representatives—prove themselves entirely refractory to even the suggestion of syntactic treatment, since they are not mental functions but physical facts solidly placed in the outer world and as such not amenable to conceptual manipulation. Nor can it be said that specimens, samples, and instances, again beyond challenge as representamina, could possibly be combined with anything else while they stand before us as instructive members of their class.

It is perhaps less obvious that visual representation in painting and sculpture is also normally without a syntactic dimension, for one is apt to recall how often likenesses are made into tools for conceptual manipulation. It will be found, however, that when this occurs, as it does in hieroglyphic writing, the images shown are complete in themselves as likenesses and therefore as representamina, before the grammarian proceeds to combine and thus to impose his rule upon them. The transformation of the image into a sign is then made by the same process which governs the reduction of other entities to a semantic status, to wit, by the suppression for the duration of their activity as a sign of all that does not serve the simple business of identifying them. The resemblance of hieroglyphic signs to the objects and activities whose concept they are to convey is therefore a hindrance rather than a help to the reader, because it tends to lead his thought into representational rather than semantic channels. The consequence is well known to any student of ancient history: Hieroglyphic systems—Egyptian, Sumerian, and Chinese—have shown a tendency to degenerate, if this is the proper word to describe what happened, into systems of abstract signs divested of all that did not contribute to their diacritical distinctiveness. As soon as they outgrew their prehistoric stages, these civilizations, except for the Egyptian, felt the need of paring down their scripts and thus of adapting them gradually to the syntactic demands of their own spoken languages.

Whatever other seemingly syntactic elements may be discovered in the pictorial arts, they will usually be found to depend on the literary prototypes from which a given subject is borrowed, rather than on the form this subject takes in concrete works of painting or sculpture. It may happen, for instance, as it did in the Middle Ages, that a painter must reproduce on one scroll a whole succession of events, which he may link together by placing them on one continuous stretch of ground and allotting to each scene a position analogous to its place in the time sequence. In this manner the spatial order can be used to signify a temporal one. It is obvious, however, that a work of art thus conceived contains no true syntactic element, in spite of its similarity to a literary narrative, since we can "read" it only in terms of spatial proximity and of the successive eye movements that it imposes upon the observer. It is only when we pass from the work of art to the tale which inspired it, as we must if we are to understand its message, that natural categories give way to that interlocking of logical and grammatical rules which alone can be called syntactic.

The same holds true of all works of art which convey a nonspatial meaning in spatial terms, whether that meaning be laid down in literary form or merely suggested as a possible way of expanding the concentrated visual statement by reiterating it in broader linguistic terms. Such an expanded statement is necessary as an aid to understanding whenever a group of figures is brought together to convey a comprehensive allegorical truth, or whenever their order is dictated not only by their natural relation to each other but by the requirements of a conceptual hierarchy. It will always be found, however, that it is the interpretation, not the work of art, which possesses syntactic properties.

What it lacks in grammatical and logical cohesion, the visual work of art compensates for by the operation of two integrating factors, one of which organizes its aesthetic surface while the other helps to bind it to its meaning. They are the unity of space and the relation of the action represented to the subject. We cannot here concern ourselves with the laws of spatial construction (which are the domain of Gestalt theory) except to say that the basic proximities in a picture must usually be interpreted in terms of a convention informing us how to read their rudimentary evidence. Only later in this essay shall we return to these so-called representational conventions, in order to learn how to distinguish them from their semantic counterpart, to which they bear a superficial (though deceptive) resemblance.

It is all the more important to gain at least a rough preliminary understanding of the relation of a visual work of art to its subject, for that relation is the guarantee of its unity of action and as such is closer to its heart as a representational unit than is its spatial arrangement; when there is a conflict between space and action, as may happen when figures are ineptly or incoherently distributed, it is always the recourse to the subject which furnishes the decisive evidence for a correct exegesis. Even seemingly irrefutable spatial affinities will then have to be disregarded, if they run counter to an established coherence of interpretation.

It is essential for our understanding of the difference between syntax and representational articulation to realize that the unity of action in a picture is due to the unity of its subject, which can be conceived only as a comprehensive totality: "the Gods of Olympus," "Achilles killing Hector," or "the history of Achilles before Troy"—to spread the argument over subjects of varying size and complexity—are all units complete in themselves and dominant over the details they imply. It is not possible to subdivide them except by transforming them into so many independent subjects, of which each in turn can become the basis for an appropriate work of art. They are then broken into aggregates of loosely related units, which may be arranged into series. Artists who find their subjects too extended in space and time to be assembled inside a single confining frame can thus evade the conflict between their task and the conventions to which they adhere by breaking their subjects into convenient discontinuous entities.

It is clear, at any rate, that there is nothing in the pictorial arts which corresponds to the linkage of small, almost adjacent units accomplished through the syntax of language. The representational units of art, figures or entire compositions, are either set side by side bluntly and without any connection except that afforded by their literary explanation, or they are given as totalities. In the latter case, which is the usual one, the subjects have their own configurational qualities independent of and variously related to their visual manifestation.

Of the remaining characteristics of representation which set it apart from sign function, one is so elementary and so deeply imbedded in an accepted manner of speech that a mere mention of it should suffice to convince us of its legitimacy. We are accustomed to say without further thought that a representamen—likeness, sample, or attorney—"stands for" or "stands in place of" what it represents, and we mean by this that it enjoys a certain permanence sufficient to assure us of a long glance at it and of an opportunity to study its message. To be sure, the function of a representamen may be limited in time, as in the case of the attorney whose duration in office may be circumscribed by his brief, but it will always be found to be extended enough to give scope to our dealings with it. If the inner qualities of the representamen are to be appreciated, we require a given time for at least a superficial acquaintance.

Signs behave otherwise, for they live by their own transience, forcing us to grasp them with lightning rapidity and then to proceed to their referents. To say, as is sometimes done, that they also, if taken singly, stand for or in place of what they point to, is to endow them with qualities which they do not possess and which are reserved to representamina.

It should be noted, furthermore (and this completes our list of comparisons), that representamina, unlike signs, exhibit a very clear-cut distinction between what they are and what they do, or, if you will, between their substance and their function. They are not, as signs are, even temporarily identical with the work they perform. It is impossible, therefore, to say of a representamen, as one does of a sign, that its mere presence elicits its referent, as the presence of smoke elicits the thought of fire; for to permit such a manner of speech, representational capacity would have to be one with being. It is not the sole fact that the lawyer stands before us which makes us experience him as a representative, nor does the meeting of a picture with an interested spectator endow it automatically with its imitative capacity. No, it is the lawyer and the picture themselves who represent, and they do so by virtue of ascertainable qualities, actions, and intensities which they bring into the process. These attributes are conceptually distinct from the being of the representamen, even if they are spread over all that is visible of it, as they are in statues and pictures. All the more will this be the case when the representative engages in his activity only sporadically, as does a lawyer or ambassador, bringing to his work just those chosen qualities which he expects to help him in achieving his purpose. Even samples and specimens, although representative only to persons prepared to take them as such, conform to the universal pattern by acting in virtue of certain qualities which correspond to the line of approach practiced by their investigators. If someone were to submit a sample to an inquiry extending to successive groups of characteristics, in order to exhaust what the sample has to say about its class, such an inquiry would never come to an end, since no aggregate of qualities can add up to constitute a being.

It must be said finally, although we are not prepared to deal with this now, that distinctness of substance and attribute is required for the particular connection that exists between a representamen and the entity for which it stands. If there were no ascertainable qualities through which a representamen entered upon its function, there would be nothing to sustain that kinship through which it points toward its principal.

It may not be amiss to reiterate in closing that the distinction between signs and representamina is supported by linguistic usage, which, although never conclusive, is always welcome as an ally in any argument about principles. We saw that representational terms are amiss when applied to signs taken singly. Language looks no less askance upon any attempt to transfer terms taken from semantic relationships to representatational contexts. It is adamant against any spurious claim that there is something like meaning or indication involved when we speak of legal representatives, forbidding the introduction of these terms into basic propositions dealing with ambassadors and lawyers. Although less dramatically, it also discourages the use of semantic expressions in connection with likenesses, which, strictly speaking, cannot convey a meaning unless their methods are allegorical and their intent, accordingly, is linguistic. Only when the representational relation is disturbed by an unintelligible detail or by one which refuses to fit itself into the total pattern do we use the term "meaning" with ease. In answering the puzzling question of what such a visual fragment may "mean," we presuppose, however, that the word has here a more than semantic significance, purporting to deal with the relation of a part that has gone astray to the whole that comprises it.

Substitution

It will be necessary, at this point, to change the direction of our inquiry in order to occupy ourselves with a function which, although distinct from representation and inferior to it in logical status, is yet so intimately akin to it that it is able to insinuate itself into most representational relationships. Substitution shares with representation its semipermanence, the separation of being and function, and the prominence accorded to its exponent, once the latter is in the position of replacing its referent. Precisely in those areas where sign function is most clearly antithetical to representation does substitution exhibit its most striking affinities with representation.

It would seem inevitable that two functions which resemble each other so closely should be intimately allied. But although related in their manner of action, the two functions do not belong to the same order of being, for substitution is a natural function and representation is a mental one. It is impossible to conceive of a representational event without implying in the very thought that there is an observer for whose benefit the process unfolds, and without whose presence it could not take place, since he is required to direct it through the application of his mental categories. Even when a likeness exhibits its beauty before an empty room, or a political representative his oratory before empty benches, the implication is always that there must be an observer whose presence is hoped for or remembered, and who attends the performance immaterially as an intellectual ghost.

Not so in the case of substitution: a machine part replaces another that has been worn out, a body cell one that has died, an atom a group of others in an organic molecule, even if there is or can be no one to witness the event. Processes of this kind are prior to the mind observing them and as such belong to the same world as any other material event which may be reported to us by our senses. Failure to recognize substitutions will therefore not alter the fact that they have occurred.

Signs alone share with representamina their mental character, for they, too, are dependent upon their interaction with a mind, only they do not usually demand an imaginary observer when a real one is absent, since it is easy for most of them to fall back upon their presemantic status as sounds, visual entities, or natural events. Signification, in turn, has a definite relation to substitution, just as representation is, as we shall see, in a sense a sublimation of it. We can explain signs, at least their more primitive types, as substitute stimuli meant to replace the objects to which they draw attention, and thus to arouse in the observer a response analogous to that which would have occurred had he been confronted with their referents. That substitution is in fact more elementary than either of the two functions with which we are here concerned, is thus proved by the simple fact that a few mental steps suffice to reduce either function to the level of substitution.

Representation may be said, then, to hold a middle position between its two sister functions, one of which resembles its manner of operation while the other shares its mental character, a dual relation which manifests itself in the peculiar dialectic governing the function of representamina. We saw that signs are by nature mere steppingstones toward awareness and as such lead the beholder beyond themselves toward the entities meant or indicated. Of substitutes the opposite may be said. To the observer they seem to eclipse the entity replaced, as they thrust themselves into his presence. Only in representation do the two contrary tendencies meet, since it puts its exponent into the foreground expecting it to be scrutinized and appreciated, and yet demands from the observer that he be ready to pass through that which confronts him toward that which is revealed by it. We shall explain at a later juncture how this connection between the exponent of representation and its principal is made.

Since substitution is a natural event, it must have a field of application different from and in some ways exceeding the orbit of specific human concerns. It is impossible to acquaint oneself with the laws governing substitution without drawing into the discussion natural occurrences of every kind, which in one way or other profit by or proceed through its agency. As practiced by man, substitution is only a continuation and in a sense an extension of principles imbedded in the functioning of nature. Hence it is not feasible, when dealing with it, to try to draw an all too neat distinction between independent physical systems and those, physical and intellectual, in the forming of which man happens to have taken a decisive hand.

We suggested in passing that substitution is at work on the subatomic, as well as on the mechanical and organic levels. It should be possible to generalize this observation by fashioning a comprehensive philosophy of nature which would choose substitution as one of its key words. It would be the task of such a philosophy to show how substitution enters the context of essential scientific thought. It would point to the incessant process of replacement which preserves the outer shells of atoms, since every electron which has fallen from its orbit is immediately replaced by one from another level or from outer space. This philosophy would show how organic chemistry illustrates the concept of substitution by indicating how groups of atoms in a molecule replace others equivalent to them, altering the molecule's chemical properties. Or, finally, it would try to demonstrate that the metabolism of animals and plants is yet another large-scale process of mass substitution, more complex, to be sure, than the others, since it involves the transformation of food into living tissue, yet essentially of the same kind. This philosophy would sum up its findings by stating that the dialectic of being and becoming which we know to be woven into the very fabric of reality is made possible only by the processes referred to, which assure the persistence of relatively permanent structures by allowing them to rejuvenate themselves from materials which the tide of time deposits upon their doorsteps.

A distinct and convincing picture of the world would

thus arise. Nature would stand revealed as a dynamic aggregate of interlocking and contending systems, each striving to replenish itself through the assimilation of foreign materials and thus to maintain itself among competitors. The peculiar dialectic of strife and coexistence, which is usually attributed to organic life alone, would have to be extended to nature as a whole.

It is important to note, however, that such a philosophy of universal substitution is possible only on one rather far-reaching assumption: it must be granted beforehand that nature is indeed composed of separate self-regulating systems, whose tendency to preserve themselves is prior to the fate of their parts. Only if we believe in the existence of such permanent, though fluid, structures, in which the loss of elements is offset by the binding of others in a continuous process of interchange, can we say that substitution is at work. We are then entitled to speak, for instance, of a tissue in an organism substituting for another that has been destroyed. If we abandon that assumption and conceive of a living being as a mere network of undirected causes, then the concept of substitution becomes inapplicable. All that we can then claim is that the disturbance brought about by the failure of one tissue, upon whose functioning the body was accustomed to rely, leads to certain changes in its co-ordination, which in turn promotes the activation of a second group of cells. There can be no substitution in a purely mechanical world devoid of closed and self-regulating systems.

A general lesson can be learned from all this. We gather that substitution takes place within a context, a framework of dynamic relations into which the substitute must fit itself or be fitted and within the compass of which it is to perform its task. We gather further that the activity of the substitute is meant to promote the interests of a totality encompassing it, whose preservation and inner balance are at stake and may be jeopardized unless those elements which have ceased to respond to its demands can be promptly and efficiently replaced.

It is possible to transfer these results without essential change to man-made substitution by demonstrating that there is always a comprehensive system, mechanical, economic, social, or artistic, which stands to profit by it. The reader will have no trouble in formulating examples of his own. We shall help him by pointing out that the replacement of a machine part serves the maintenance of its normal level of production; or that the replacement of an amputated leg with a wooden limb assures a man's continued physical balance and mobility; or, to chose an example in which man himself plays the part of the substitute, the replacement of an actor by his understudy assures performance at the stated time, no matter what the state of health of its leading actor.

It will be noted, however, that, although they may be very close, it is not possible to equate man-made substitution with its natural counterpart, since the first is distinguished by the presence of a factor which we cannot discover in the second. In man-made substitution the overriding interest, for the sake of which the transaction takes place, will always be found to be divided between man and the creation whose continued integrity and usefulness he has set out to protect. To him, substitution is always, in a sense, a means to an end, which it is impossible to understand, therefore, unless one is prepared to take into account the aims it is designed to advance. Even if undertaken for genuinely unselfish ends, as it is when a surgeon sets out to replace a vital human organ with its mechanical equivalent, substitution is not only at the service of a cause, but indirectly also of the person laboring for it.

When a situation requires not the maintenance but the resolution of a *status quo*, this human element will come to the fore. It is prominent in the solving, through substitutional methods, of a mathematical equation that has refused to yield to more direct methods of approach; and it will become obvious in the simple but instructive case of a man who decides to resolve a pressing situation by substituting one method of locomotion for another, and who jumps on a horse when his car has collapsed, in order to be in time for an appointment.

As we pass from what may be called the conservative phase of substitution to the more dynamic varieties, there is a definite shift of emphasis from maintenance of the *status quo* to concern about man's own ends. The system within which substitution occurs retains its relative importance only as long as it can be regarded as reasonably permanent and autonomous. As soon as the system is looked upon as unstable enough to invite man to modify it in the pursuance of his own goals, it begins to yield its autonomy to him. If, instead of repairing the objects in his employ, man is compelled to reject and replace them in their entirety, then he himself becomes the sole beneficiary of the transaction. For the afore-mentioned person who refused to be frustrated by mechanical failure in his car, neither his technical nor his natural conveyance were more than extensions of his own body, to be exploited for the sake of speed.

It must be added, in order to complete this argument, that the standards of adequacy to which a substitute is asked to conform are also determined by the purpose guiding its activation. It is not always true, as a frequent manner of speaking would imply, that the substitute must necessarily labor in the position of a mere stopgap, a temporary expedient inferior by nature—or made inferior by abuse—to the object replaced. This may be the case. It is equally possible, however, that a process of substitution may come to pass because man, instead of merely trying to preserve by using whatever surrogate may come to hand, may have a desire to improve or to resolve. We have discussed the case of mathematical substitution, without which certain equations may defy all efforts at analysis. It may be equally to the point to remember that the voyager, upon whose resourcefulness in the face of emergency we commented, may reverse the direction of his action by taking up mechanical locomotion instead of conveyance by horse, and thus improve his speed. It will depend upon the total situation in which he finds himself, whether, given complete freedom of choice, he will prefer to abandon his horse for a car in order to follow the invitation of the road, or whether, in primitive conditions, he will rather switch back to the animal conveyance of a pre-technical age. Whole civilizations, in fact the entire human race, have engaged in progressive substitutions of this kind. We need only multiply the figure of our voyager by the number of persons involved in the technical revolution of our own day in order to obtain a measure of the size of those substitutive events which occur when a sector of mankind is prompted to forsake its old tools for other instrumental equipment.

One other possible misconception should be corrected. It may be tempting to give an all too literal interpretation to the terms substitution and replacement by postulating that in such a transaction the substitutes must retain the same locale where their forerunners labored before them. This is not the case. Topographical precision will be necessary only in rigid mechanical systems such as man-made machines, in which the space to be occupied by each part is calculated in advance, and may neither fall short nor be extended. Usually, however, function takes precedent over topography, so that a substitute will satisfy if it merely succeeds in fulfilling the task bequeathed to it. The exact spot where its work is performed (provided only that it be done within and in the service of the system) is a matter of only minor importance.

It is also the survival of the whole that determines which entities are to be admitted as substitutes and what functions they are to perform. Not every object that finds itself in the vicinity where another used to be is rendered acceptable by the mere fact of its presence. It is also required that the delicate balance of the system which acts as its host not be upset when the stranger from the outside proceeds to make his home in it. The potential substitute will be a foreign body, and as such is unwelcome as long as it fails to co-operate. It may so irritate or encumber the organism which encloses it that the latter will die unless it succeeds in expelling the intruder. Only if what we may call the substitute raw material is first transformed into suitable organic substances before it is invited to contribute to the whole, or if the organism changes its tonicity, can the foreign matter be utilized.

The process is by no means exclusive to living beings, although because of their marvellous inner richness and complexity they are the prime examples of it. We may take another instance from recent history: modern war, we will recall, may throw great numbers of bewildered civilians on the battle field, where far from being desirable replacements for trained men in uniform they contribute to defeat by impeding operations. Yet with a further change in the fortunes of war these very civilians may be utilized as replacements in a last effort to stem the tide. As part of an "organism" whose tonicity has changed, they will have to attune themselves, as best they can, to the demands made upon them in the face of impending collapse.

The question now arises as to how, given the existence of the kind of system described, the survival of the whole can determine appropriate performance by its parts. Such a performance will rarely be automatic, since the substitute may be too inert to undertake its task unprompted, and since, if it possesses the will to shape its own destiny, it may actually balk at the function imposed upon it. It will be necessary, therefore, that the system be provided with what may be called "determinants," entities so endowed and distributed that they will be able to direct potential substitutes to their work and to steer their energies. Such determinants will be expected to possess greater permanence than do those entities whose temporary fate they control, since they must stand out in the flux of replacements. About their nature no generalization can be made except that they must possess the energy and "managerial" capacity required to regulate the flow of replacements; furthermore, if there are several of them, they must be so attuned that they will be able to engage in frictionless co-operation in the common task. A mere thrust of energy, if sufficiently potent, may constitute such a determinant in elementary physical systems. As entities become increasingly differentiated their internal determinants will tend to respond to the challenge of this complexity by developing their own specializations, until they will seem to constitute systems within systems, with their own methods of action and interplay. In the living cell the nucleus, and within it the genes, circumscribed structures of high complexity, are responsible for the even flow of metabolism. In human society, where the individual is the smallest unit, the worker will function as a determinant. The organized effort of many and their interlinkage in one great chain of specialized skills will be required to effect such internal substitutions as the continuous supply of merchandise.

It must be added that not all man-made substitution is internal in the sense alluded to, since man may use his ingenuity to provide systems external to him with his energy and directives. We speak then of dependent systems, knowing that they are incapable of furnishing their own determinants and thus must obtain them from the outside. Man surrounds himself with mechanical and electrical contrivances which, having only a very limited ability to regulate themselves, would be bound to run down and get out of order were it not that the repair man or maintenance crew stand ready to provide them with substitute parts. Even self-regulating entities such as the human body may deteriorate to the status of a dependent system when it becomes necessary to assure their survival through the supply of external substitutes for normal organic functions.

We are now in the position to discuss the manner in which substitutes may be said to operate, a topic which we have deferred, since we cannot deal with it intelligently without presupposing what we said about their relation to their systems. We have seen that substitutes, like representamina, function by virtue of certain chosen qualities and intensities which we declared to be distinct from their being. It is now possible to specify what these ingredients are. Substitutes will activate only those among their potentialities whose excitation is demanded in the interest of the whole. Other potentialities which they may possess will remain in a dormant and ineffectual state; they constitute, as it were, a realm of privacy into which the public business of the substitute function will not be able to penetrate.

By stating the reasons why a given substitution is to take place, and the functions which it is to perform, we imply what qualifications are demanded from any candidate for substitution. To take an example from human life: A man may replace another because he holds a similar job, because he is a member of the same social group, because he speaks the same language, because he possesses a trained intelligence, or merely because he is a healthy creature of flesh and blood. In each instance the qualities raised to prominence correspond to a definite type of demand, which in turn will be determined by a system, commercial, intellectual, or military. The fate that awaits the human substitute will depend on the kind of organization that reaches out toward him and thus upon the qualities he has to offer to it.

The degree of kinship that governs the relation between the substitute and the principal will also be determined by systemic requirements. Some systems, such as machines, will not be effectively supplied unless the replacement parts to be fed into them agree with their predecessors in a great number of physical properties. Other systems may allow more latitude, particularly since the common possession of qualities such as weight, durability, or chemical affinity may outweigh kinship in the sense of the more familiar types of classification. Such systems offer a choice between what we may call close or remote substitution, the latter often a mere makeshift, resorted to because the hope of finding truly adequate replacements has been abandoned. Clearly there is a sense in which a substitute may succeed or fail in filling the place vacated by its predecessor. The more remote it is in type from its principal the greater the chance that it may not be able to measure up to minimal requirements.

No liberation from the compulsive demands of physical systems will occur unless man asserts his autonomy and breaks the hold that causality has upon him by passing from the realm of fact to the freedom of make-believe. When at play and thus relieved of the restraint which the laws of practical life impose upon his actions, man is capable of replacing any object by any other, so long as it can be manipulated in a manner analogous to the modus operandi of its principal. The playing child, when really immersed in his activities, will find no difficulty in forgetting the categorical distance between his toy and the object with which the toy is temporarily identified, simply because he postulates an equivalence between the actions brought to bear upon both. By substituting one mode of behavior for another closely akin to it, the child is able to overcome the difficulty which would otherwise prevent the mutual replacement of the objects concerned.

Even those restraints which the limitations of the environment impose upon the practice of make-believe will disappear when the mind, the freest of all determinants, engages in substitution in order to test a theory, creating hypothetical situations and inserting various components into them. Although the relationship of the factors in such a game may be remote, the experiment may succeed nevertheless, since all things, to whichever universe of discourse they belong, possess some points of comparison on the basis of which substitution can be attempted. If the result of the experiment should be absurd or otherwise unacceptable, this in itself will contribute to the lesson learned.

We shall emphasize in closing that substitution is not without a very trenchant moral implication if applied to organic beings and particularly to man himself. Man's dignity can be profoundly and adversely affected by his use as a surrogate, since subservience to a system implies disregard of the rights of those involved in it, if these rights are not in harmony with the interests of the system. If necessary, the system will stretch, reduce, and distort the pattern of individuals caught in its machinery, treating them as means to an end, to be used and wasted upon command. As a principle of human organization, substitution has a tendency toward totalitarianism, since, like the latter, it has little regard for human values.

There is no difference, so far as their treatment is concerned, between the human substitute and his principal, for both are subject to the same limitations and possible indignities, since they must submit to the directives issued by the same determinants and through them submit to the dominance of the system. Indeed the description which we gave of the position of a substitute in a system might be extended to any entity functioning as part of a dynamic order. To be replaceable without loss or regret is no less a degradation than to serve as a replacement.

Nothing could highlight better the gulf that exists between substitution and its nobler sister, representation, despite their great functional similarity, than the contrasting attitudes involved in the process. Far from degrading those who participate in it, representation enhances their standing. It is an honor to play the role of representative, whether as an attorney, deputy, or parliamentarian. And just as the degradation implied in substitution may be visited upon proxy and principal alike, so representation in improving the position of its exponent glorifies the entity for whom he stands. To be representable is to hold definite political and social rights, of which the citizen may be proudly conscious when he exercises the privilege of the ballot. Hence one of the severest penalties which society can inflict upon one of its members is to deprive him of his honor as a citizen by declaring him ineligible either to represent or to be represented.

What holds true of legal representation applies also, in spite of some modifications, to its other variants. No artist ever chooses a subject for his work without the conviction that it embodies values which justify his efforts, nor can a spectator study and enjoy the fruits of the artist's labors without becoming aware of the importance of the subject represented and of the values which the artist found in it. We must note, however, that, unlike legal representation, which depends on the status of the principal, its artistic counterpart operates without regard for such formal considerations, since its only purpose is that of realizing the potential values woven into the fabric of its subject. The theory of representational value involved in this distinction will have to occupy us later.

v   *Vectorial and Adaptive Substitutes*

As we consider once more the ethical implications of substitution, we arrive at an important observation which we have allowed to go unrecorded, although it is implied in what has been said before: Whenever an entity, of whatever kind it may be, enters a system as a substitute, it is immediately deprived of its uniqueness as an individual and treated as a member of a species whose characteristics make it desirable as a contributor to the common cause. It is always *a* machine part, *an* organic substitute, *a* piece of food that is required for the maintenance of a system, and it matters little what other characteristics the object may possess if only the required generic qualities be present. It is the same quality which the system demands from all of its members, including the one whose place the substitute is to assume. It could not be otherwise, for to say that something is a unique individual is to assert that it cannot be replaced, since its logical position puts it above any attempt to break down the barriers of its originality. When we said that substitution degrades the individual caught in its meshes, we had in mind this reduction of something unique, calmly at rest in its unchallenged individuality, to a mere aggregate of qualities, each of them a point of contact with a species.

It will be necessary to remember this fact as we turn our attention to another modality of substitution, which treats the substitute not as a means to an end but as an end in itself, an object of desire for the possession of which we may exert all our faculties. No such substitution can take place unless both substitute and principal respond to the same human drive, which can be appeased only by the attainment of its aim; a drive which like all human urges, instincts, and propulsions, is directed toward a species and thus fulfills itself by treating all individuals it encounters as samples of their class. We need only remind ourselves that to the hungry an animal is not a beloved fellow creature but food, or that to the sexually starved a woman may be a personally indifferent promise of satisfaction. Instincts cannot stop to consider the individual qualities of their objects. Even the desires for home, family, and security, which presuppose the uniqueness of what they seek, actually aim at a general condition, although the condition is impossible to satisfy except through the presence of certain individuals. The great divide between man as an animal and man as a spiritual agent lies precisely at the point where such drives give way to the appreciation of individual value, as sexuality gives way to love, that profound immersion in the uniqueness of another person.

It is the relation to a drive which connects the kind

of substitution now under discussion—vectorial, as we shall call it—with that similar transaction which merely reshuffles instrumentalities. We saw that substitution of means can only occur if the constituents of the whole are given direction and meaning by their orientation toward a human aim. The same applies to vectorial substitution, which aims at giving vicarious satisfaction to a pre-existent drive and thus, in its way, is also a means toward an end. Only when there is more than one drive competing for our attention, no matter whether simultaneously or successively, does substitution refuse to come to pass, since the situations then created are entirely foreign to each other and mutually incommensurable. They would not be if it were possible to substitute one human drive for another. But this extreme assertion of human freedom is prohibited by the limitations of our nature, which permits us to steer, utilize, or suppress instinctive utterance, but not to manipulate and control it arbitrarily.

There is, however, another kind of freedom which vectorial substitutes do derive from their relationship to a drive. They are independent of those immediate, pressing wants which prescribe the activation of many other substitutes whenever the absence of the factors to be replaced threatens the collapse of a system. Instead, vectorial substitutes often seem to create the desires to which they correspond, bringing proclivities to light which otherwise would be overlaid by demands of the day. The drives to which they offer vicarious satisfaction are always present as potential appetites, waiting to be aroused by appropriate stimuli. Thus the entities which correspond to these appetites may appear to produce spontaneous and novel reactions in the persons exposed to them, although in fact they only release latent tendencies.

The results of this insight are far-reaching. For if it is true that vectorial substitutes tend to assume the guise of primary incentives, then we must face the possibility of losing all criteria by means of which we could distinguish between their pretensions and those of their principals. We will at times be able to recognize substitutes for what they are only when they carry a mark upon their faces, betokening their permanent and, if you will, professional inferiority to original phenomena. Even if they display the imprint of their vicariousness, there will be a temptation to pass them off for that which they are not, by practicing deception either upon unsuspecting observers, who may never find out what has been done to them, or even upon ourselves.

Deceitful and illusory as vectorial substitutes are, reality provides us with plentiful examples of such entities. There is on the human scene an abundance of mannequins and dummies, of fictions, shams, and counterfeits, all intended to play as best they can upon our credulity and to hoodwink us if there should be a gap in the armor of our vigilance. All of these depend on deception, since they can assuage desire only if they have been able to carry off their fraud. If they have not, if we become aware of the falseness to be foisted upon us, we remain dissatisfied after we have experienced what the surrogate had to offer us. We will compare its service with that which we would have expected from its principal and find it wanting. Victimized by a frustrating experience not of our making, we are likely to be indignant about the deception perpetrated upon us. Even when we use a vectorial substitute knowing it for what it is, and without illusions about its status, satisfaction will come only if we resign ourselves to not receiving what we wanted to have.

There are two ways out of this logical and moral impasse, both of which mankind has taken and exploited to the full. One of these has been discussed before. It is always possible, as we saw, to change the moral implications of vectorial substitution and to enhance its creative possibilities by retreating from its rigid alternatives into the freer realm of play. The playing child does not deceive himself about the truthfulness of his assumptions when he treats a thicket as if it were a castle, a wooden stick as if it were a horse, or a playmate as if he were an enemy Indian. He knows that these substitutions are only pretenses, valid as long as the enchantment lasts and to be cancelled as soon as the grown-ups call him back into their alien world. He will immerse himself in the make-believe that his own activity has created, without ever regarding it as anything but fictional. Because of this, and because the rules of reality are, as it were, suspended for the duration of his play, he is able to carry out any substitution that his fancy dictates without ever meeting the conflicts that beset the practitioners of vectorial substitution on an adult plane. We must not believe that the child's activity leads to far-reaching perceptual adjustments between the objects of his fiction and the toys by means of which the fiction is brought about. They remain very largely what they are and yet enter freely into the context of his own imagining.

The second avenue of escape from the dilemma implied in vectorial substitution leads into representation and thus into our central field of interest, which we are as yet only circling from afar in order to mark the boundaries separating it from kindred functions. Our ig-

norance compels us to be brief. It is possible to overcome the fraudulence of vectorial substitution by confronting the observer with an object that, while similar
to its principal and thus a possible tool of deception, yet
makes its character known through the manner in which
it presents itself to us. Sculptures and paintings are not
easily mistaken for what they represent. The artist lifts
them out of their environment by enclosing them in
frames and hoisting them on pedestals. Not content
with this external separation from the scene of our
everyday activities, such works of art tend to draw attention to their otherness by letting the material of
which they are fashioned shine through the form imposed upon it. They are marble, canvas, and paint in
addition to being battle scenes or Greek divinities.

As a result, works of art have an advantage over
vectorial substitutes in that they need be neither makeshifts nor lies, since they lay no claim to being real in
the sense in which we attribute reality to the things of
our practical environment. They do not pretend to be
what they represent, because they only embody it. It is
paradoxical but true that the strangely discordant and
equivocal function of vectorial substitution finds the
resolution of its internal conflicts in being absorbed into
representation and thus being placed above the level of
its own duplicity.

Works of art have the additional merit, compared
with vectorial substitutes, of permitting the replacement of an individual entity by another, which shares
with it its uniqueness and the values adherent thereto.
Paintings and sculptures are not the duplicates of their
subjects precisely because the material out of which
they were made, and the manner in which it enters into
the impression created, prevents them from being classi-

fied with their principals. They possess a degree of independence from their prototypes which mere effigies or dummies cannot boast. As a consequence we can afford to enjoy and judge them as individual achievements, for they stand upon their own merit as portrayals, without being drawn into the sphere of their principals. Their subjects in turn suffer no diminution of their individuality when likenesses of them are made, since these preserve their categorial distance from them.

We omit the frequent cases of a statue or a painting being used as an effigy or of the latter, when removed from its original context, being appreciated for its aesthetic merits, since such cross-references between human functions would only serve to confuse the issue. It must be emphasized, on the other hand, that we cannot extend the principle expounded to other than artistic matters without laying ourselves open to absurdity, since any effort to duplicate what is unique is bound to be in vain. It is in this light that one must judge the magic practices frequently observed in the lower spheres of life, practices meant to influence the fate of an individual by taking vicarious action upon his substitute: the singing of an incantation over a wax figure in order to make a lady yield to the attentions of her lover, the killing of an enemy through the device of piercing his effigy or, in a way, the shooting in paleolithic caves of the painted image of the game-animal desired. It is true that the absurdity of such actions is in part due to the unwarranted belief that their performance, if undertaken according to a pre-established code, has a mysterious long-distance effect upon the person or creature envisaged. We must note also, however, that unlike the analogous action in games, whose fictitious character is always retained, this substitution occurs in the world of fact, and thus proclaims its own futility. It is possible, after all, to engage in similar magic procedures without expecting distant persons or objects to feel their influence, as is the case when a crowd, under the impact of political passions, is deluded into burning an enemy leader in effigy. Few of those who participate in such mob action will believe that the hated antagonist has actually fallen dead only because a straw man, with the enemy's name written on a label, has been committed to the flames. The absurdity remains, however, since it should have been understood that the substitution is prohibited by the uniqueness of the entity replaced. The only result that such vicarious action can produce—and obviously the one usually aimed at by its instigators—is a momentary release of pent-up tensions and perhaps a redirection of volitional capacities. The effect is necessarily transient and subjective.

We turn to the last and perhaps most important variety of substitute, which we may call adaptive, since it reflects and fosters the adjustment of an organism— the human in particular—to its changing position in its environment. There is only one category of such substitutes; they are usually called mental images. It is clear that these, if they fit into this discussion, must be bracketed with what we called professional substitutes, since they possess no standing except that which they borrow from primary phenomena. They have the same tendency that we observed in other entities of their kind, of usurping the place which cannot normally be conceded to them and pretending to be what they are not. When the usual controls have lapsed because a person is asleep, drugged, or insane, then such images tend to gain the upper hand and to usurp the place of his normal environment; they will be reduced to their usual status only when consciousness returns and re-establishes the proper proportions of things.

About their native insufficiency there can be no doubt, for even when they reach the intensity of hallucinations they never have the completeness nor the clear-cut and unquestionable identity which we are accustomed to observe in objects of the external world. It is as if the principle of individuation did not extend to them. We find therefore that mental images, no matter whether spontaneous or deliberately evoked, always remain vicarious and hence unsatisfactory to the fully conscious person. He will not be able to overcome the elusive and fragmentary character of his fantasies unless he resolves to endow them with the body which they lack by projecting them into the outer world, re-enacting them in plays, reliving them in his literary activity, or stabilizing them in the materials of the visual arts. Only if he succeeds in this endeavour can he be said to be in real possession of the fruits of his inner life.

We hasten to add, before we say any more about a notoriously treacherous subject, that we do not mean to pronounce the entire human production of mental imagery, which is believed to accompany our waking and sleeping hours, as substitutional. It may well be that there is a purely spontaneous stream of imagery which furnishes the raw material to the correlatives of our drives. Images of an ornamental or abstract character like those called "hypnagogical," which visit us when we are drowsy, may well belong to this primary kind, as may those which possess and fascinate the drug addict when he is under the influence of his intoxicant. It is certain, however, that most mental images are, as we said, correlatives of drives, and as such are tinged with a substitutional quality even if their profile is so weak and their content so vague that they cannot furnish the organism with more than the most elementary directives. It is difficult, in fact, to conceive of drives as something more than a mere undirected expression of physical discomfort and of the unrest pursuant upon it, unless we presuppose that they receive their guidance from a mental image, no matter how ill-defined. When directed toward a goal, as they always are in man, such drives plainly need intermediate steering, which helps them to discover the satisfaction desired.

If such gratification fails to materialize because the objects of our interest belong to the past or future, because they are far off, difficult of attainment, or forbidden to us by individual or social sanctions, then the mental image receives a heightened function, since it is made to compensate us for that which did not or could not come to pass. It will then take the place of experience and provide the organism with vicarious enjoyments or fears, because real ones have failed to manifest themselves. It is clear that such images play an important part in the life of a creature such as man, whose nature compels him to transcend the position in which he happens to find himself and to reach into the distances of space and time, dimly or explicitly aware of a world surrounding him. The incongruity in the status of a creature whose limitations are at odds with its power to project its interests, is bridged by this device which permits the organism to retain its balance, although the orbit of its concerns surpasses by far its physical competence.

Psychoanalysis has acquainted us with those substitutional images which reflect unsatisfied desires: dreams of the day and night, in which man experiences that which he cannot or dare not bring about. The less he is ready to translate the irresponsible wish into action, the more vivid the colors of the images. Most daydreams have a clear-cut substitutional character, for they tend to cast the dreamer in the role of the chief actor in a scene that has been expressly posed for his glory, the satisfaction of his ego or of his sexual desires, a scene whose blatant impossibility feeds upon its hypothetical character. The dreams which visit the sleeper are very much more complex than these, since beside the drives of which he is consciously aware, others, more deeply hidden and imbedded in a long forgotten past, may be simultaneously at work in him.

We need not take sides at this juncture in the dispute over Freud's original thesis about the interpretation of dreams. Suffice it to say that in our opinion no single category of drives is likely to be responsible for the creation of a phenomenon such as the dream, which is marked by the coexistence and interpenetration of the most diverse unrelated entities. It would seem that any interpretation claiming more than dogmatic validity would have to do justice to its subject by approaching it on several levels of thought.

Compensation for unsatisfied drives, however, does not exhaust the substitutional function of mental images, for we find this function at work whenever man's consciousness expands beyond his immediate surroundings to an awareness of the larger context within which his actions unfold. What we may call cosmological imagery is a correlative of the convictions by which an individual regulates his conduct, and as such is no less important in heralding the pattern of his personality than are his more intimate fantasies. Such images are all the more significant since the individual usually receives them from his cultural environment, so that their choice, character, and intensity can serve as a measure of the degree to which he may be said to be integrated in his community. A society that lives by a central creed imposes upon its members very definite images pertaining to the events which attended its foundation, the supernatural guarantees for its continuity, the hopes and fears which it projects into the future, and the general shape and pattern of the universe. These articles of faith will be laid down in religious documents and recited at the appointed times, and many of them will be given visual form in pigment or stone.

There is a strong relation between these communal expressions of belief and the intimate imagery of any person living within their sphere of influence, since it is impossible to escape their impact. It is one of the most important functions of religion and of religious art to regulate man's imaginative life, to discipline it by providing it with archetypes, and thus to exert an indirect influence upon his impulses. Not content with excluding from their official imagery any but man's central concerns, religious sages tend therefore to present that of which they approve in a stereotyped manner, aware that only repeated experience of the same representational pattern will really anchor it in man's consciousness. There may then be a complete correspondence between internal and external imagery, as there is in the tantric religions of India, which pronounce the identity of mental images and idols and make of their fusion in the mind of the celebrant the central event in his devotions.

When there is a certain tolerance for novel visual types, as there was in Europe in the high Middle Ages, then art and mental imagery may fertilize each other. Many of the devotional subjects then invented received

their impetus from visions which in turn were often derived from expressions used in the liturgy.

It is certain, at any rate, that no civilization can
preserve its hold upon the minds of its members unless
there is a common stock of images, religious or patriotic,
that is engraved on them. It is a symptom of the disintegration of a civilization if this treasure of common
experiences and certainties begins to fall apart, laying
the individual open to the often irresistible assault of
his own drives. When communal imagery falters or dis-
appears, the gap is bound to be filled by images of a
different and chaotic kind, which proceed from an undirected and unreconstructed inner life.

At this point we must return once more to the discussion of vectorial substitutes, in order to note the
relation that many of them have to our drives and mental images. It is possible to project the fulfillment of our
desires into the outer world without abandoning its
vicarious character, aware that we cannot or would not
undertake the translation of the wish into inexorable
reality. The result is either magic or play. The action
of the sorcerer who tries to win a lady in her absence
through incantations is of course a vicarious fulfillment
of a wish and as such closely akin to that shortcut
through reality which is the lure and danger of daydreams. That children's games are also, to a certain extent, anticipations of desired situations in which the
children wish to participate is suggested by their choice
of themes, which are almost always taken from the life
of grown-ups and very often, in the case of boys, from
heroic and picturesquely wicked deeds. The enormous
strength of a child's drives and desires, which only the
mature person learns to moderate, finds an outlet in
such activity which allows him to live through the situa-

tions created by his fancy without having to undergo their realistic implications. As a result, games must be held within their own sphere by prohibitions keeping the enactment of fancied situations from passing into reality. Many of them would degenerate into unadulterated savagery, causing tragedy and sorrow, if the drives that find expression in them were not stopped short before they reach their goal. They must be kept in their own domain of make-believe reality through the promulgation and acceptance of a set of rules.

Mental images and vectorial substitutes, being more than means for the repair of existing deficiencies, have in common the ability to stand for anything that can become the object of a drive, including the nonexistent and the unattainable. Drives have a tendency to vest their objects with impossible, synthetic perfections, endowing them with a glittering ideality that no substitute can ever hope to match. When such ideals are not embodied in existing objects, as they are in the early phases of human love, the result may be a permanent and fretful dissatisfaction with life which no real experience can cure, since it will always be regarded as a poor substitute for that which did not come to pass. The makeshift world of the confirmed idealist becomes bearable only if he learns either to appreciate the greater perfection shining even through the humblest phenomena or to turn his gaze from the things which cannot suffice him toward a reality beyond. Only then will the object of his drive cease to be an idealized member of a species and reveal itself as a truly irreplaceable individual.

VI *Replicas*

We have now taken a glance at the principal varieties of substitution and would be ready to turn to a discussion of representation were it not for the fact that there is yet another form of relationship, that of the replica to its duplicate, which must be considered first. The bearing of this problem upon the subject of our central interest becomes apparent if we keep in mind that a work of art, in addition to representing a given subject, may also be a replica of another work of art, either because it is a copy, and thus probably inferior to its prototype, or because, as a member of the reproductive arts, it is the equal of other facsimiles.

What do we mean when we speak of replicas, and how do we distinguish them from genuine representamina?

It is tempting, of course, to try to cut the topic

short by insisting that anything is a replica which bears the hallmark of similarity to something else, and that the discussion of the subject will resolve itself into one on the nature of resemblance. To this we must reply that we cannot solve our problem by conjuring up a function as little understood and beset by as many difficulties, philosophical and psychological, as the concept of resemblance.

We will leave this matter untouched, since it belongs very largely to Gestalt psychology, and shall only insist that a complete description of replicas will also have to take cognizance of their dynamic aspect by conceding that they are what they are only because some active agent gave them their identical shape. It is impossible to think of replicas—machine parts, row houses, coins, prints, performances—without introducing implicitly the figure of their maker, or at least the substratum of forces by which they are brought into the world. Even the members of a species of plants and animals can be called replicas of each other only on condition that nature itself, which brought them forth, be conceived as a spawning matrix of life which heeded a dark creative urge when giving birth to swarms of analogous creatures. Without this background, this prompting by a powerful determinant, resemblance alone would not suffice to make replicas out of near-identical members of a species.

We can go further and say that since there can be no replicas without an artificer who fabricated them, their creation must answer a purpose and fulfill at least a potential need. We shall heed this aspect of their nature by defining them as identical substitutes, waiting to serve as future members of a system and to satisfy its expected identical requirements. Replicas are thus neither makeshifts nor improvements upon precedent, as

are the other types of substitutes, since it is their task
to hew as closely as they can to a predetermined line.
Their intimate mutual resemblance allows them to take
each other's place without causing appreciable changes
in their systems. Conversely, it is possible to make a
whole supply of replicas—say machine parts or machine-
made merchandise—before the need for them arises, because we anticipate that the system or systems into which
they are to be fed will always make approximately the
same demands. When there is no such continuity, because a system is itself involved in dynamic change,
replicas will be useless or out of place.

It is thus possible to predict under what circumstances replicas are likely to be serviceable. We expect
them to fulfill a useful task when supplied to rigid mechanical systems such as machines, whose movements are
always the same and which, when run down, will therefore require identical repair parts. We may expect,
furthermore, that replicas will be handy as vectorial substitutes, since the organism directs its desire or interest
toward all members of a species and thus is likely to be
satisfied by any of them. Since the drives in question
are always potentially present, waiting for a sufficient
stimulus, they will be equally aroused through any
replica which may present itself.

By assuming furthermore that all men have approximately the same fundamental needs, it is possible to
lay the logical basis for a mass production that will
throw great quantities of identical merchandise on the
market, in the expectation that they will be absorbed
when human nature responds to their identical lure.

Finally, replicas can be regarded as the lowest common denominator in different but equivalent substitutional situations such as those which occur when legal

exchange is offered for the purchase of merchandise. Coins and other kinds of money are among the most typical replicas because there must be an identical tender in situations of exchange, capable of being converted into and measuring the value of any commodity. If money were not standardized in appearance and value, there could be no assurance of receiving a readily recognizable countervalue for delivery, and the economy would be thrown into confusion.

It is instructive to see that this classical kind of replica is also a universal substitute, the only one that can be put in place of anything within reach. It is capable of this universality because its value is not intrinsic but nominal, having been determined arbitrarily on the basis of its intended relation to the economy. The loss of individuality, which is the typical fate of substitutes, and its replacement by purely functional and utilitarian categories, could not be more graphically illustrated than by this admittedly extreme case. No wonder that being convertible into money and capable of being bought, no matter at what price, also involves a loss of quality that makes the entity thus traded fall from its rank as an individual to that of an exchangeable commodity.

Not all replicas stand in a transitive relation to each other as do those which we have considered so far. There are also those, much more notable from our point of view, which have somehow lost their equality, having been entirely overshadowed by their prototypes and which are, in consequence, reduced to the humble status of copies.

To understand these let us construe a hypothetical case. We shall take our start from the commonest of commonplaces by reminding ourselves that, according to a popular phrase, one egg is like another, so much so that it is usually impossible to distinguish between them. In saying this we imply that according to our definition a basketful of eggs cannot even be regarded as a heap of genuine replicas, since there was no intelligent purpose involved in their creation.

It is possible, however, to transform the members of this particularly uniform species into copies or dependent replicas by making a few gratuitous assumptions. Suppose that we were all members of a religious community worshipping the Easter bunny as its totem animal; suppose, furthermore, that this mythological creature had once condescended to lay one single egg of the general appearance of those which are brought to our breakfast tables, and that this egg was now enshrined and worshipped as a unique guarantee of fertility, welfare, and continuity; then, obviously, all other eggs would become humble, dependent copies of the one distinguished by its cosmological significance. The equality reigning between the members of the species would be entirely upset, and replaced by a condition in which all eggs produced under usual circumstances would be weak, material reflections of their mythological prototype. The unique mode of its creation would lift the latter out of the range of irreverent comparison, endowing it with an aura that mere naturally-begotten eggs will never possess, and causing their subordination to their sacred paragon. Somehow, the existence of the primeval egg would be conceived as the cause and reason for the existence of the others, whatever the precise moment when the Easter bunny made his gift to the world. If there were eggs in ages preceding this original confirmation of fertility, a magical anticipation would stamp them as replicas of the as yet unlaid bunny's egg.

Nor would the eggs of earthly creatures be the losers in this cosmological transaction, for their prototype would irradiate them with its subtle influence, giving each its share of reflected glory, and thus raising it beyond the status of material things.

Why all this would come to pass it is not altogether easy to say, undeniable as these various implications are. It should be remembered, however, that replicas are not necessarily members of systems, and that they thus need not fulfill those criteria of usefulness to which all members of systems must conform. Since replicas are very similar to each other, as are all members of closely integrated species, they can be distinguished only if one of them possesses a strong nonmaterial characteristic setting it apart from the common crowd. We might add that the close imitation of something that is by nature unattainable and incommensurable, as is the prototype of a series of replicas, puts the copies in a position analogous to that of a person who follows a leader but does not succeed in overtaking him and thus remains forever dependent on his guide. The combination of physical similarity with dissociation of value can thus be regarded as the cause for the unequal status of replicas. It seems to account also for the overflow issuing forth from the archetype and for the manner in which the archetype bathes its duplicates in its own glory; for to remain within the metaphor, the steady servant of a leader finds the reward for his humility in the reflected rays of greatness which long association may cause to gather upon his head.

The uniqueness of the archetype makes itself felt in the care with which the circumstances of its creation are recorded, whereas it matters little how its replicas came into the world, since each of them derives its fundamental being from the existence of its paragon, and the latter must have a definite location in space and time if its individuality is to be assured. Even when nothing is reliably known about its place in the historical sequence of events, as would be the case with our example of the cosmological egg, a vague assumption of such timing must prevail if the archetype is to retain its superiority over its replicas.

On the other hand, the first-born among a series of replicas does not automatically become their superior archetype unless its claim, if made, were to be confirmed by a concurrent uniqueness of value. The first in a series of row houses, for example, even if all the others were patterned after it, could not rank as a prototype in the sense here defined, unless it were appreciated as the original and unique creative utterance of its architect. It may rank as such to a small coterie of acquaintances ready to appreciate his personal accomplishment but not to the public at large, which judges homes only in relation to its own needs.

The ordinary concept of causality as applied by common sense to our everyday affairs must suffer a few modifications when we extend it to replicas. When we said that our hypothetical primordial egg was the cause for the existence of all that was to come, we did not, of course, mean to imply that it was linked with other eggs, past and future, by that chain of instant reactions which we have come to associate with the idea of causality. The relation is a "magical" one, rather, and thus does not exclude the purely natural origin of ordinary eggs through the usual insemination and growth, if only what we may call their essence be derived from their superior prototype. There are of course replicas whose life lies entirely in the historical dimension, such as copies after artistic originals, which cannot but be posterior to the masterpieces after which they have been fashioned. In other cases, however, such as the one we construed, the time relation of an original to its replicas remains indefinite. It is even possible, as we shall see, to have replicas by anticipation, provided only that the same ultimate originator be responsible both for them and for their subsequent paragon.

Whatever their specific relation to their prototypes, dependent replicas must take their place in the time sequence in a manner befitting the fact that their model occupies the only fixed point in an otherwise undifferentiated series. They are always replicas by anticipation or afterthought, and thus differ from equal replicas, whose mutual relation in time is immaterial.

It must finally be emphasized that we cannot conceive of the archetype of a group of copies, any more than of a series of equal replicas, without adding the idea of the maker who brought it into the world by a creative act. The archetype tends to concentrate upon itself all the historical interest which, were we dealing with equal replicas, would be spread over the series as a whole. It matters greatly to his devotees, to speak in terms of our illustration, that it should be the Easter bunny, the great demiurge and principle of creativity, who chose his time and place to deposit his single gift in a grateful world. When, how, and under what propulsions the individual chickens which followed his example made their respective contributions matters no more to the members of our hypothetical cult-community than it does to those who live by other persuasions. We are justified, at any rate, in saying that the differential value which lifts archetypes of the kind discussed above their dependent replicas is extrinsic to them, since it is founded upon the circumstances of their creation, and the prestige enjoyed by their creator. Because it is impossible to reproduce this historically-determined set of outward circumstances, their presence assures to the archetype a uniqueness that may not be borne out by its own innate characteristics.

Where, then, do we find dependent replicas of the type described? After what has been said, we may anticipate that they will be most numerous in the field of religion, which more than any other human interest guarantees the incommensurability of replicas and prototypes and postulates for the latter its origin in a creative act.

There is, in fact, the category of sacred objects that have been hallowed and set apart by virtue of their connection with a miracle or with the life of a saviour or saint; objects whose uniqueness would be sufficient unto themselves were it not that the demands of a spreading cult-community required their duplication in other localities. The process that ensues diverges somewhat from the example which we gave, for unlike the indifferent mass products of fertility the man-made replicas of sacred objects are themselves revered and experienced as endowed with qualities akin to those of their prototypes. The irradiation with reflected glory, which we recognized as the reward for imitating the inimitable, is then usually strengthened and confirmed by an act of consecration, which in turn transforms each hitherto dependent replica into a source of potency and thus makes of it an original on which other replicas may depend. A great chain is created, every link of which derives its strength from its predecessor and imparts it in turn to its sequels, dotting the earthly landscape with places in which the divine presence has been actualized.

Nor is it sacred objects only—memorials, tombs, symbols, and relics of all kinds—of which these observations can be made, for it is obvious enough that the sacred acts of the ritual are also frequently conceived as repetitions (although not always identical ones) of a founding act by which they were instituted. Fundamental problems of the Christian liturgy, problems over which churches have been rent in two and heretics have left the common fold, are predicated on the question of what, in a solemn re-enactment, constitutes a dependent replica: whether the founder's act is merely imitated, in reverent devotion to his memory, or whether it is actually repeated in its old identity whenever the liturgy is performed. The first is the attitude of early Christianity, which looked upon the sacrament of the Eucharist as a memorial action illuminated by the afterglow of the event celebrated; the second is the later Catholic belief, according to which Christ's body is really present—no less than it was when Christ spoke the founding words—whenever the bread is broken and the wine imbibed. Let us note, however, that this second interpretation of a sacred act, which makes of it the equal of its historical prototype, is possible only because an act of consecration has taken place that lifts the object of the cult above the level of the usual replicas and thus enhances the significance of the actions attending to it.

Religious art shares this emphasis upon the relation of archetypes and their similes. The unique esteem, for instance, in which certain icons were held by the pilgrims who traveled long distances in order to prostrate themselves before them is expressed through the creation of numerous copies intended to bear testimony to a cherished experience and perhaps to a prayer answered. These images—e.g., the Madonna of Altoetting or the Virgin of Le Puy—all have a legendary founding history and an unalterable location on the religious map, and thus present themselves as true prototypes in the sense defined. They are never without a specific architectural setting which accentuates their individuality. The copies, however, which were made after them, remain anonymous and without epoch, as they appear in almost any setting, ecclesiastic or secular, and thus help to spread the fame of their miraculous prototype over the countryside. Each of them enshrines, as a reward for its humble anonymity, a spark from the glory of the original.

The principle here exemplified has a wide field of application in religious art. It is, in fact, well known that periods dominated by theological values were inclined to regard existing works of art as the only legitimate source of inspiration for the artist, thus surrounding the copyist's labor with an appreciation which other periods have tended to deny to it. The medieval painter, for instance, would choose as the starting point of his pious exertions what was then called an "exemplum," a prototype whose value was assured by its age or by some religious connection which rendered it venerable. Around this core he rallied his creative forces, ready to surpass the old standard to the extent that tradition permitted and the full employment of his powers on God's behalf demanded. Given favorable circumstances the work of his hand in its turn was capable of achieving the status of a prototype upon which later generations of artists would rely, so that it would take its place in a succession of mutually-dependent replicas reaching far back into the early centuries of Christianity.

As recent research has shown, many of these strands of tradition took their start in works of art that derived their worth from association with a great religious event or personality. The frescoes in the Church of the Ascension in Jerusalem, St. Jerome's illuminated copy of the New Testament, the mosaics in Justinian's Church of the Holy Apostles seem to have radiated their influence through the centuries, begetting works of art which even upon a manifold remove show distinct traits betraying their origin. It is natural, under such circumstances, that iconographic innovation in the Middle Ages was frequently due to the combination, in one work of art, of details derived from various sources— a circumstance that has proved of great help to scholars in their task of reconstructing lost, distant prototypes from groups of replicas partly and variously related to them.

Early in the history of Christian art the further discovery was made that the relation of the artistic archetype to its copies could overcome the theological opposition to images of persons and scenes so holy that any portrayal of them in a material medium was apt to be condemned by zealots as blasphemous. The prejudice against the representation of sacred events inherited by Christianity from the Jews tended to assert itself whenever there was reason to remember the Old Testament injunctions against idolatry. All the more welcome to the defenders of images were the legends, spread early with an obvious end in view, which established the existence of so-called "Achyropoieta," authentic likenesses of Christ and of the Virgin Mary said to have been made during their lifetime. St. Luke's reputed portrait of the Madonna is the best known of these. All of them have been the source of likenesses made and revered in later centuries.

It is thus certain that the relation of the respected artistic original to its copies has not only a pedagogical function in the training of future artists, although nobody would venture to deny this, but also an important religious mission. It would seem likely, in fact, that the regard in which classical works of art, particularly of the High Renaissance, have been held in modern times, is a late and secularized version of the older attitude toward religious prototypes, abetted by the exaggerated esteem now bestowed upon the supposedly godlike powers of their creators. For we are in the habit of attributing the uniqueness of outstanding works of art to the singular states of insight which had guided the artist in conceiving them. There is this difference, however, between religious copies and copies after works of art esteemed for aesthetic reasons: the latter are apt to be undertaken in emulation of their exemplar rather than in humble acceptance of it; for every incipient artist must hope that he will pass beyond that formative stage during which he must be guided by imitation of famous prototypes, to the state of maturity when he can dare to be original because his technical equipment will have begun to match his growing powers. He knows that the universe of artistic invention is never closed, unlike that of religious evidence, which can be augmented only through a sudden, unlikely, and unpredictable act of God.

It must be added that dependence upon "exempla," which we had occasion to note, did not prevent the medieval artist from being creative to an extent rarely paralled in the history of art. He thus presents the latter-day analyst of his work with an intriguing contradiction be-

tween the methods of the past and their results. We believe that this formidable paradox can be resolved by
applying our findings about the nature of dependent
replicas and remembering that their archetype is incommensurable and beyond approach. An age as acutely
aware of this gulf as were the Middle Ages, and convinced that nothing short of an act of consecration could
possibly bridge it, would have good cause for limiting
its imitative efforts to the retention of significant traits,
since that complete equality could never be attained.
The advantage to be reaped from this attitude was that
the artist, inspired by his contact with the incomparable,
was given scope for creative utterance without fore-
going the lifegiving relation to the past.

It has been shown, for instance, that, in contrast
to later periods which engaged in much more exact
visual quotations, the Middle Ages kept their copies of
famous buildings at a considerable formal distance from
the prototype. The various churches of the Holy Sepulchre in Western and Southern Europe, built to recall
the far-away memorial in Jerusalem, share with their
model only certain selected features, in one instance its
circular plan, in another the distance between the col-
umns or the measurements of the inner sanctuary, while
all remaining details of plan and structure were left to
the discretion of the architect. As a result, these replicas
of a famous architectural monument form a remarkably
diverse group held together only by the common allegiance of its builders to some kind of centralized plan. In
one telling instance the relation of a structure to its
prototype was expressed only through the retention of
the same name in the act of consecration, without any
recognizable formal similarities.

The most extreme case perhaps of the mentality

described above is the development by the Fathers of
the Church, and by their medieval successors, of the
so-called "typological parallels"; that is, the arbitrary
combination of Bible passages which bear some casual
resemblance to each other and thus could be construed
as proof that God meant to foreshadow essential features of the new dispensation in the old. Thus the Cru-
cifixion was believed to have been "prefigured" in the
hoisting by Moses of the brazen serpent—with the ele-
vation above the earth as the basis of comparison—or
in Jacob crossing his arms as he imparted his unequal
blessing to his unequally beloved sons. The Resurrection
of Christ after three days was thought to be foreshad-
owed by Jonah's involuntary stay, for the same period,
in the whale, and his subsequent deliverance.

That these combinations, though arbitrary and artificial, resulted in the creation of a network of archetypes
and dependent replicas, is beyond doubt. It must be
noted, however, that the discovery of replicas by this
method was so far removed from the paths of ordinary
experience that it became the privilege of the learned,
who knew how to lift the curtain from the secret of
Divine intentions. Only the fact that Christ himself had
used some of the comparisons from the Old Testament
to signify his foreknowledge of his own impending death
could justify such a procedure. It was concluded from
this that God, the great determinant, had decided to
conduct the course of human history in the period of the
Old Covenant in such a way that those who knew could
discover in it a figurative forecast of events to come in
the reign of the New. To speak in the terms developed
in this book: the existence before the time of Christ of
certain dependent replicas, similes of future actions and
events, was to be taken as proof of the truth and reality

of their prototype. It throws a strange light upon the methods of thought involved in such speculations that the replicas in turn could only be perceived as such if prior knowledge of the nature of their prototypes was available.

The system of typological parallels is, in short, a closed and self-justifying one and thus inaccessible to outside argument. It can be entered only through the gateway of faith. Once accepted, however, by admitting the authority upon which it rests, it blossoms forth into a colorful multitude of similes, parallels, and replicas, which have a tendency to propagate themselves and thus to cover history and even nature with their borrowed splendor. The believer trained in establishing such relationships, which know of no verification or weighing of evidence, will have his pious labors rewarded by finding the central tenets of his faith reflected wherever he may turn his gaze.

We hope not to be regarded as irreverent when we add that the system of typological parallels, one of the mainstays of medieval theology, bears a curious and revealing resemblance to a very modern theory, which, we submit, requires from its devotees a similar intellectual submission through an act of faith. Just as in medieval theology God manipulates history so that the knowing will recognize its relation to subsequent events, so, according to Freud, does the sovereign unconscious arrange for the enigmatic display in our dreams of visual shapes which only the analyst will understand in their relation to basic human drives. Analyst and scholastic thinker are enthroned as interpreters of similarities so deeply hidden in apparently heterogeneous events as to be beyond discovery by the uninitiated. Both types of learned men operate by separating what seems significant to them from the flux of less important phenomena, acting as arbiters over what is to be admitted into their thought. They will both be tempted to admit everything, since there are no criteria of exclusion, and thus to transform the entire world of their knowledge into a vast exhibition of dependent replicas.

Psychoanalysis, in its original form, is, in brief, a self-justifying system based on faith in very much the same sense in which this could be asserted of the typological speculations of medieval theology. It reveals the true character of this doctrine that its defenders are always ready to charge their opponents with being antagonistic because they are the victims of compulsions and delusions defined in Freudian terms, so that even those who would take their stand outside the system are forcibly incorporated into it.

It is certain, at any rate, that both the psychological and the theological doctrines mentioned above are complete and self-sustaining, whether or not we assume that there ever was or will be an observer capable of interpreting what a sovereign determinant has decided to undertake. The process of deriving replicas from their prototype is unqualified by any regard for a public. It possesses no direct reference to the usual means of cognition and can be unraveled only by inspired insight.

As we glance back at the types of replicas we have examined, it becomes apparent that they have certain traits in common which we have as yet failed to emphasize. Those entities which we may call religious and quasi-religious similes carry the negative distinction that little attention needs to be paid to the business of rendering them as similar as possible to their prototype. There should be, to be sure, a certain modicum of resemblance. But while in artistic copies this similarity is a criterion of success, it is in typological parallels no more than a minimum condition for the establishment of a preordained relationship. In the latter case, therefore, an increase in similarity does not necessarily imply a closer approach between original and replica, since both are conceived as equidistant at all times. There are no "good" or "bad" copies among typological parallels, no more than there are among architectural renditions of the Holy Sepulchre, as long, at least, as the religious attitude prevails. If their status ever changes, it will be because they have come to occupy a different rank within the system of values of which they are part: We repeat that a dependent replica can be made the equal of its prototype by performing over it an act of consecration.

Artistic copies, on the other hand, are predicated on the belief that, given appropriate conditions, they should be able to replace their original, no matter how great its innate superiority over them. The conscious effort of the copyist to emulate the masterpiece before him implies that, for the moment at least, he does not regard it as something so far above his own powers that any attempt to approximate its effect would be futile. The work of art he copies seems important to him not because of the unique circumstances of its creation but because of its inherent value, which he will try to recapture if he has the required skill and self-confidence. Only the historian or the connoisseur, or the artist in a critical and reflective mood, will realize the enormous gulf that separates even the best imitative effort from the never-to-be-rivaled creation of a master.

Before we close, a few words must be said about those systems of replicas which either depend on a prototype whose existence is only postulated, or which help the prototype to come into being. The first is true of the various Neoplatonist cosmologies. Plato himself had taught that the things which we know are no more than imperfect material replicas of immaterial ideas, of cores of being, which contain in themselves the essence of the world's far-flung multiplicity. It is instructive to observe how this rudimentary doctrine was developed by pagan and Christian Neoplatonists into an ever more comprehensive theory, which drew the Divine Creator Himself into its orbit and explained the manner in which material things had been evolved out of their superterrestrial prototypes. It was believed by now that the ideas were the nuclei of God's creative thought, and that the process through which they were impressed upon shapeless matter was accompanied by an irradiation from above that made the things thus formed forever reflect the glory from which they came.

These ambitious cosmologies clearly revolve around the concept of the dependent replica, whose religious implications they expand into an image of cosmic events. The theory postulates therefore not only the ideas themselves, which Plato had assumed in order to explain the existence of abstract species, but also a determinant who had called them into being, and a process which induced the adherence of all dependent replicas to their prototypes, and through them to their maker. The irradiation with a golden light, which we used as a simile for the influence of the archetype upon its replicas, appears here literally and visibly as the agent of divine penetration without which the material replicas of God's thought would be unable to achieve distinctness and being. The whole system is mystically revealed and the philosopher is a seer privileged to interpret it.

Though the Platonist philosophy postulates prototypes, because the beauty and rationality of the world would be inexplicable without them, it is the privilege of the theatrical producer and of the persons working under him to create prototypes through patient manipulation of their antecedent replicas. The rehearsals, through which a performance takes shape, can only be understood as rather humble replicas of the public event which they help to prepare, and toward which every detail of acting, staging, and lighting contributes. The spectacle that is to be, with its elegance, its tense atmosphere and public expectation, sheds its rays in advance upon the efforts made to prepare it, and these in turn receive their justification from their future prototype. A determinant is called for in the figure of the producer or director, who controls their relation to their prototype, since only he can know his own intentions and thus relate the preliminaries to the final event. He looks upon the necessary rehearsals as the sculptor does upon his models, which are also antecedent replicas meant to try out and prepare a future work of art.

It should perhaps be said finally that there are relations between prototype and replica which imply the theoretical and logical possibility of putting in place of the archetype one of its identical facsimiles. Such relations occur whenever the model employed is a purely numerical and quantitative one, so that it can be made to coincide with its equally quantitative replicas. The Paris meter, for instance—surely a true archetype, considering its unique historical and geographical associations—is the common standard for all identical measures, because these are defined by postulating a congruence of length that would be observed if they were laid side by side with their original. It is assumed that any other meter used anywhere in the world could be put in

place of the one deposited 160 years ago in the Paris
Pantheon and would be found to coincide with it. We
should not be too surprised to discover that an archetype so easily replaced, which owes its rank to an arbitrary definition, would have little of the incommensurable value and compensating radiance which we found
involved in the relation of other prototypes to their dependent replicas.

VII *Categorical Representation*

The reader will have become aware by now that, however close nonrepresentational functions may come to those of representation in some respects, and however easy it may be at times to confound them, there is a definite barrier which separates representation from the functions investigated so far. It is as if a new horizon were opened, a new dimension disclosed when we leave the consideration of substitutes and replicas and begin to occupy ourselves with our central problem.

Representation, in contrast to everything we have studied until now, is not only a mental function (a title that any subjective image can claim) but also a rational one, and thus partakes of the rule of laws which is the distinctive characteristic of rationality. It will, in fact, be our chief task to discover the nature of these laws, which have been unduly neglected for the sake of an analysis of logical and semantic rules, merely because the canons of representation happen to be without the rigidity that distinguishes the former. At the present time in history, when so many of the most stringent laws have been found to be merely the accumulated results of great numbers of freer relations, this insistence upon the most sterile facets of experience is not to the credit of the thinkers concerned.

We shall begin by analyzing the structure of what we propose to call categorical representation—the relation of a sample or specimen to the class for which it stands —in the hope that the simplest of the types involved will help us to understand the properties of kindred, more complex phenomena. Categorical representation itself will thus serve as a sample—that is, as a categorical representative—in an inquiry involving several more components of its class.

Before us is an indeterminate number of members of a species—say apples, books, or international travelers— all distinguished by the possession of common characteristics, and none of them necessarily, in the sense defined, a replica of any of the others. We choose one of these at random, concentrate our undivided attention upon it and decide to treat it as a representative specimen of its class. The question arises as to what it is that we are undertaking, and what confirms us in the belief that we are engaging in a meaningful and promising activity.

To the first part of this question most readers will be ready to give a quick and not uninteresting answer: they will insist that what we seek in the chosen specimen is information about the general nature of its species and that the choice of the specimen, given the postulated uniformity of the series, may be due simply to the fact that this particular sample was the first one at hand.

Two conclusions can be drawn immediately: first, that it is impossible to set up categorical representation unless there is an observer or an "interpretant," as we shall call him henceforth; second, that it is of the very nature of such representamina to inform, that is to serve our intellectual interests. About the first of these assertions little need be said except that the demand for an interpretant is a novel one, since both substitution and the mutual relation of replicas could dispense with his presence. The fact that it now becomes obligatory goes far in suggesting that human rationality is involved.

The second assertion is akin to the first, for its claim that we aim at knowledge when we set up representation presupposes that rational means are available for extracting such knowledge. Although substitutes and replicas may be able to teach us something about their principals because they sometimes have an intimate similarity to them, whatever information they may be able to impart is incidental to their nature. Representamina, by contrast, inform essentially and intrinsically.

At this juncture, the difficulties begin that obstruct the solution of our problem from any of the traditional and accepted points of view. For how can the connection between a representative sample and its species be a rational one, since samples and species are not parts of thought but entities in the outer world? Clearly, the sample does not indicate or mean its species, provided these words are allowed to retain a shred of their original significance, any sign relation being thus excluded. What remains, then, is the frank recognition that the connection between a specimen and its class rests upon the most obvious and visible attribute of all specimens: namely, the fact that anything, in order to be a sample, must be a part, a portion, or constituent of its class.

This is indeed a rational, even a self-evident relation, for it is impossible to think of a specimen without implying that there is a comprehensive group which entitles it to that name, provided, of course, that the class consists of more than one member. Conversely, it is impossible to conceive of a species, no matter of how indefinite an extent, without implying the existence of entities belonging to it. When we say that something is representative or typical of its class, we thus leave the inevitable inference that there are other entities not presently available, which might have been found equally illustrative.

However, categorical representation is based not only on the relationship of the part to the whole; it also demands another relationship, that which links the sample of a given class with other samples of the same class. This relationship is established by a second assumption, namely, the belief that the specimen shares with all the other examples of its class a certain undefined "essence" which makes of them what they are. By injecting "essence" into the discussion, we place ourselves at variance with certain recent trends in philosophy, which shun the vagueness and metaphysical implications of words of this kind. We must emphasize therefore that we believe it impossible to arrive at a rational understanding of representation without making use of this term. However the word be defined—and there have been many and distinguished attempts to define it in the history of Western philosophy—what matters to us is that there must be a certain intangible and yet pervasive quality which connects the illustrative sample with its equals within the species. We can make one concession, however, to the current demand for palpable and identifiable realities: this essence, as conceived by the interpretant, is a preliminary concept, designed to assist further intellectual advance as he prepares to find out what the specimen has in store for him.

Categorical representation thus results from the co-operation of two originally independent relationships: one, which we shall call the rationale of representation, is asymmetrical and intransitive, since it consists of the internal division of one comprehensive entity; the other, which might be called the basis of categorical representation, is symmetrical, since it involves the common possession, by all members of the group, of the same invisible but dominant quality. Of these the first, the relation of a whole to its parts, is a purely formal condition, incapable of predicating anything about the content to be revealed, whereas the second carries with it the rudiments of impending material disclosures. Either may precede the other in the awareness of the interpretant. It is impossible, however, to establish representation unless there be first a sense of the relation of the sample to its class. Without this rationale, which bestows order and meaning upon the underlying identities, the community of essence is an unwieldy and indeterminate concept that is likely, in its blurred and fuzzy way, to extend far beyond the area intended.

We must at this point inquire whether the relation of a whole to its parts, which we found involved in the statement that something is an illustrative specimen, can be said to be representational when applied to material totalities. Can we state with any degree of confidence that a physical part is capable of representing its whole simply by virtue of the fact that it is a part? It would not seem to us that this is necessarily the case, since bodies and systems of this kind lack one of the chief characteristics of species, namely their relative homogeneity. Unless we think of them as mere aggregates of identical and separate components—an attitude discouraged by both physics and psychology—we shall have to concede to them the possession of a definite Gestalt, a configuration, which will assign a specialized function to each component and subordinate it to the character of the whole. Without such homogeneity, however, there is little likelihood that a community of essence can be established.

There are certain exceptions to this. It is possible, for instance, to postulate a community of essence where a rational point of view would refuse to discover such a community, by introducing a certain magical substratum capable of justifying any, even the most far-fetched, relationships. It is quite feasible, on this basis, to claim that a trophy, a pair of antlers for instance, represents the whole from which it has been cut off for the simple reason that it shares in the essence or aura of "staggishness" which permeated the beast when still alive. Many hunters will be quite ready to take that attitude, though usually unknowingly. The chief reason why such trophies are taken is, however, not their representational quality, which may or may not be felt, but their very obvious substitutional function; for the part that has alone survived stands for and is a memory of the whole that perished before the hunter's gun.

There are, however, more serious and valid applications of the principle that a whole can be represented by its material part; perhaps the most important instance is the physical experiment. We shall try to be short, since the matter is somewhat extrinsic to our interest, although none will want to deny that it is pertinent, since it is the acknowledged purpose of the experimental scientist to set up an arrangement, as representative as possible, of the interplay of forces in the world at large. Only if it is, and if his results have proved valid, will he venture to proceed to the next step and generalize what he has found by inductive reasoning. We suppose then that the experiment is meant to test universal physical laws, since only then will the experimental set-up be continuous with the rest of the world and thus part of a seemingly homogeneous totality. We claim, in harmony with accepted scientific doctrine, that his results will be representative only if he succeeds in insulating the area of his test from surrounding influences so that it can be regarded as a discrete specimen of conditions independent of their locale. Whenever such tests are made, the scientist will have to disregard the organic unity of the world, the dependence of all of its parts upon the structure of the whole, since awareness of this would destroy his confidence that there are repeatable identical occurrences. The Newtonian universe with its infinite homogeneous extension in all directions and with its resultant lack of structure is thus an ideal theoretical framework for experimental science.

What is true of physical parts must be claimed equally for illustrative specimens; they, too, can function as such only when they have been properly insulated. If an example is given to us in a context to which it is so intimately wedded as to appear inseparable from it, then the context itself is made to share in its quality as a specimen. An animal, for instance, observed in its interaction with its native environment, can be regarded as typical of its species only when its environment is accepted as part of its representational capacity. Any extension of the findings to creatures living under different conditions must be excluded.

A third example—and a very instructive one—of the

representation of a whole by one of its physical parts is to be found in the relation of the parts of speech to the grammatical or rhetorical units comprising them. A single word, even a group of words, is usually not capable of representing the sentence or paragraph of which it is part, since it is no more than a building block employed in the construction of a passage and as such does not share in the total meaning of the whole. But if instead of a word you have a paragraph long enough to exhibit the style and manner of thinking of its author, and thus to share essential characteristics of his literary activity, then it will be found that categorical representation has become possible. The critic will be justified in seizing upon such a paragraph, in preference to dealing with a larger and more unwieldy whole, in analyzing its intangible essence until it becomes intelligible, and in then applying his findings to the book involved or to the author's total output. If no more than a fragment of a literary work is preserved, as is often the case in Greek and Roman literature, then the critic has no other choice than to use this method. His understanding of stylistic essence, articulate or inarticulate, will then help him to reconstruct the parts that have been lost.

We have now studied the rational presuppositions of categorical representation. It is time that we turn to the concrete events which occur when an interpretant decides to avail himself of the shortcut to knowledge which categorical representation affords. The first of these is the choice of a specimen. As long as the species is uniform, this must be regarded as a random event; it will lose this randomness only if there is prior knowledge of individual diversities, inclining the interpretant to the belief that some samples are more representative of the class than others would be. There can be no doubt that this choice of one member of a species, instead of others which might have been equally fit, if perhaps less easily available, has a strong substitutional tinge, although there is little here to suggest a makeshift or temporary expedient. It will be remembered that anything that offers vicarious satisfaction for a drive directed toward all members of a species indiscriminately must be regarded as a vectorial substitute. Categorical representamina are indeed substitutes implicitly, since the information extracted from them might have been obtained with approximately equal success from any other member.

It may even be claimed that a species should be defined as a group so constituted that any member of it, if put in the place of any other and subjected to the same methods of scrutiny, will exhibit the same characteristics. The interpretant, finding the species as a whole beyond his reach because its members are scattered and their number unverifiable, will do well to substitute for a study of all its constituents that of a specimen or group to which he happens to have relatively easy access. Anything that the interpretant undertakes because of his desire to know will then have to be classed as in a sense substitutional, not only the choice of a representative specimen but also the scientific framework for its proper utilization, e.g. the setting up of experimental gear, the stimulating of reactions or the creation of particular conditions under which the effect under study may be expected to manifest itself.

As long as the interpretant is thus actively engaged in pursuing his quest, the substitutional pattern maintains its hold over him. It is only when the information begins to come in that categorical representation is able to assert its own rights.

We assume now that this stage has been reached. The interpretant will then use the rational categories previously formulated as a framework for the concrete knowledge he hopes to obtain. When he conceived these categories as a correlate for his decision to regard a chosen object as a sample, he was not yet in a position to think of any specific applications of which they might be capable. Even the extent of the species within which the relation was to hold may have been unknown to him, so that a monkey may have figured as a sample of its own breed, of anthropoid apes or mammals, or of the higher animals generally. This curiously vague preliminary stage now comes to an end as the interpretant formulates the questions which the specimen is to answer for him.

It is important to realize, however, that the imminence or presence of concrete disclosures does not invalidate their rationale and their rational basis, which continue to function as a necessary joint scaffolding for coming representational events. They are the a priori conditions whose presence alone makes representation possible. Therefore they cannot be abolished or annulled as long as representation continues. Because of this pervasive presence of conditions that are as comprehensive as they are vague, there is in principle no limit to the kind of representational relations into which a sample may enter, so that it cannot be regarded as a valid representamen unless recourse has been taken to a complex system of checks, capable of insuring its veracity.

It is not only the extent of the species that is to be determined, for it is necessary also to determine how far the individual chosen as a sample can be regarded as representative of the species. It may, after all, be a poor specimen or an aberrant one, from whose behaviour few valid conclusions could be drawn. There is, in short, in all categorical representation a certain latitude which coincides with the mutability of the species envisaged. The research student, aware of this variability and of the consequent possibility of faulty evidence, will therefore have to try his utmost to eliminate this source of error. Starting from whatever knowledge of the species he may possess, he will exert proper caution in the selection of his specimen. If he desires a higher degree of reliability, he will be well advised to choose a group of specimens instead of a single one, because this will allow him, under favorable circumstances, to arrive at mathematical precision by the production of a statistical average. When we claim that something is well represented in a certain area—such as a species of hummingbird in the United States—what we mean to express is usually that there are many specimens available for study, either singly to individual lovers of nature or collectively for a sampling within a comprehensive statistical attack.

Many further refinements in the use of inductive reasoning may be introduced with which we are not here concerned. We cite as a single example the method adopted by social scientists who sample entire populations; they divide them into groups by such categories as social standing, age, sex, or income class, then produce the average of each, and apply the composite result to a study of the community at large. The procedure, if properly conducted—that is, without loading the evidence—has all the exactitude one might desire. However, it lacks in content what it has gained in precision, transforming the human sample from a focus of multiple potencies into a lifeless abstraction.

As we have seen, categorical representation can only reach its cognitive aim when the question to be put to the illustrative instance is specific, concrete, and articulate, for we are to gather information about a species, not merely to become acquainted with it in a general way. We are invited to concentrate our attention upon circumscribed areas in the representamen, even while our awareness of its total existence persists. As representational act follows upon representational act in the course of a program of research, there is thus a tendency to narrow down the area of interest and at the same time to sharpen the methodical tools, until the discovery of a general truth compels us to subsume all that has been found under a few simple principles. At any rate, it is no more possible to envisage the character of a species in its entirety while approaching it through the avenue of research, than it is to comprehend individual things and events through a similar procedure. Categorical representation must be selective. The student who applies it as a method will therefore remain aware that the species, with its indefinite gamut of closely-linked qualities and capabilities, is always beyond any approach he may devise, a totality which he cannot hope to reach.

We find for the second time in this study that categorical representation presupposes the inner diversity of a class or family, only that this time the multiformity is not a numerical but a qualitative one and as such inherent in every member of the species. It must be emphasized, as we finish this survey, that the species, although every act of research is aimed at a better understanding of its characteristics, remains remote and in the background as long as representation prevails. While the student is occupied with the sample at hand

and with extracting from it whatever information it may be able to yield, the problem of the applicability of this information will remain blurred, providing no more than a general aura of significance for his activity. It is only after the specimen before him has done its work that he will be able to turn his attention from the foreground of accustomed sights and problems to that dimension in depth where the importance of his results for a generic scheme can be weighed.

What remains to be said about categorical representation leads us into an area of experience far removed from the clear-cut queries and the well-sifted evidence of science, for we must acquaint ourselves also with the intuitive use of representational technique. Let us assume that we face an object—any object—and that something about it stirs in us the conviction that it is representative of its category, without eliciting the active inquisitive response of the student. Representation will then be arrested in that preliminary stage where it remains before specific problems have been formulated and a technique has been developed for solving them. There will be, in fact, no scope for outward activity, since any such release of the forces engendered by the object has been specifically excluded. Instead, the interpretant will meditate upon the object before him, he will try to penetrate into its being, to bring his own prior experience to bear upon it, and to expand his resultant sensation into a general awareness of a broad facet of experience. It is clear that his experience will have no particular aim or purpose, since it is a concentric afflatus enveloping the object contemplated in an ever-widening aura of significance. Its momentum will be emotional, and its result not an increase in knowledge, but, at best, a refocusing and concentrating of powers preparatory to further intellectual and psychological advance. Categorical representation, in this early comprehensive phase, is, in short, a germinal and central experience from which new orientations may originate. We shall anticipate later definitions by referring to it as categorical symbolism.

It is characteristic of categorical symbolism as a mode of experience that it always takes its start from an individual entity, with all its idiosyncrasies and imperfections. If scientific representation at its best is statistical and thus tends to exclude divergent qualities, its symbolic next-of-kin revels in the acceptance of singularity. Categorical symbolism takes its normal start from the isolated instance, not from the representative group. Only in the somewhat unusual case of the art historian and of other scholars working with the criterion of style are whole groups of entities—such as pictures or sculptures—taken as a point of departure for an analysis that must not detract in any way from the uniqueness of the specimens concerned. It is part of the methodical difficulty of the history of art that it cannot disregard the individuality of the objects falling under its competence, while it is also obliged to subsume them under groups and to regard them individually or collectively as representative of historical tendencies.

With respect to the single categorical symbol, we note that insistence upon its individuality produces an unusual linkage between the unique and the generic; the multiplicity of far-flung instances is concentrated in this one present example, which retains its specificity while its being envelops them all. In a sense, therefore, its uniqueness and the idiosyncrasies pertinent thereto enter into the representational process, showing how the essence of numerous extraneous objects or events is embodied in this one intransmutable occurrence; or conversely, the uniqueness of the symbol, which stands for related instances, is living proof that everything, no matter how seemingly alike, partakes of the God-given quality of individuality. Since this is true of the members of one species, so the voice of experience insists, it must be true of the world at large.

It goes perhaps without saying that the rationale of representation and its rational basis are as clearly present in this arrested stage as they are in its subsequent scientific phase, with the difference, however, that there is as yet none of the gradual revelation that later research may yield, so that these a priori categories hold the field alone. As a result, and because they have foregone their preliminary function, these categories acquire an almost material consistency. Essence seems to become tangible, like a permeating fluid; and the relation of the part to the whole, originally a logical one only and therefore without spatial connotations, begins to show some characteristics of extension. As the interpretant meditates upon the specimen before him, images of related entities may seem to cluster around it. The species itself, originally no more than a mental construct and as such without shape or articulate design, seems to round itself out and to acquire the character of a configuration. At the same time—and this would seem a contradictory attribute—the species loses its definite logical extension, since there is nothing in the unguided contemplation of the single specimen that could serve as a criterion of the range to which its lessons could be applied. Open in all directions for the admission of groups of kindred entities, the species melts away into indefiniteness.

When the class is known and yet the example is re-tained in its unchallenged singularity, then a state of symbolic consciousness is reached in which rational con-siderations regain part of their weight. There is then a correspondence between individual characteristics in the specimen and similar ones known to exist in its class, with the understanding that the sample may exhibit in sensible concentration what only protracted analysis or long experience would discover in the principal: the vir-tue of such an arrangement being that what previously had been diffuse and abstract has now become palpable and manifest. It is thus possible to attach long trains of speculation to the characteristics which the interior of a streamlined railroad car shares with the whole of Ameri-can technology, of which it is a typical example: its em-phasis upon speed and upon visible function at the ex-pense of other forms of beauty; the display of wealth by means of the materials employed; the fact that the car is available to all, if only they can afford the price; the unconcern with which travelers entrust themselves to the technical knowledge of an unseen and unknown engineer—these and other obvious characteristics con-nect the single exponent of a technical civilization with its unwieldy and unattainable totality.

It will be observed that it is still the individual in-stance, in all its arbitrariness, which serves as a starting point for the experience described. Not content, however, with giving himself to the rapt contemplation of an un-differentiated totality, the interpretant is now seen to prefer an analytic approach, engaging in a procedure comparable to that of the social scientist, who counts up the results extracted from various social groups and transfers them to the community at large. Only this time the conclusions are qualitative, not numerical, and derived from meditating upon an intelligible entity—our neon-lighted and chrome-plated railroad car—not from keeping accounts on an aggregate of independent groups. Most important of all, the sampling of populations serves the acquisition of knowledge not previously available, and thus is a scientific undertaking, while the contemplation of a categorical symbol only confirms and drives home what is already known.

We cannot leave the subject without pointing out how deeply its application affects the creation and appreciation of works of art. It will be remembered that pure categorical symbolism comes to pass when representation, instead of being released into active inquiry, is stopped short and held captive in its contemplative phase. At this stage, then, there is no cross-reference between the senses and thus no testing of the reality of what has been encountered, with the result that the representamen stays suspended, unconfirmed and uncontested, as an aesthetic phenomenon. There is, in other words, no really valid dividing line between real occurrences and works of art, so long as both play the role of categorical symbols, for then both belong to a realm beyond scientific truth and falsehood, where allusion to previous experience takes precedence over verification.

It will be found, however, that, although their status is equal, works of art are superior to real objects and events in their ability to suggest symbolic experiences. To Western man, untrained as he is in the harnessing of his inner powers, categorical symbolism comes as a chance occurrence, neither expected nor contrived, and dependent on an incalculable combination of mood and circumstance. It may attach itself to any object, although living and natural things may enjoy a certain preference. Since nature operates without regard to the structure of human consciousness, no prediction can be made as to when the occasion may arise that will set off the experience of categorical symbolism.

This is not so in the case of works of art, for they usually are so slanted that certain types of experience will almost impose themselves upon the beholder. Because of the freedom the artist enjoys in moulding the raw material of experience into entities expressing his beliefs, some facets of life will be omitted and others emphasized as he works on the creation of a consistent interpretation. The spectator is invited, accordingly, to expand the evidence of his senses into a general awareness of artistic truth, to bring his experience of life to bear upon it and thus to gain the confirmation of insights which but for the agency of the work of art might well have stayed forever subliminal. What had been only vaguely adumbrated by the disorder of everyday concerns is thus cleansed of its dross and brought to consciousness. A new focus is attained.

We do not believe, however, that, quite apart from the scale of artistic rank, every work of art is capable of providing us with the experience of individual truth generalized, for in order to render this possible, the starting point must be a realistic portrayal of individual entities. An idealized art such as that practiced by the Greeks and postulated by Aristotelian aesthetics will not be able to achieve this, for it aims at what should be, not at what is, and thus embodies in its formal alignment that generality which is to be the subsequent contribution by the interpretant. Its very perfection shuts it out from the benefits of categorical symbolism. It creates images which we may admire, or toward which we may want to rise, but in which we do not recognize ourselves. Nor can it be said that those linear types of art which in the past have been the handmaidens of religion —such as the art of the Ancient Near East or of the Early Middle Ages—are intent upon categorical symbolism, for it is their aim to show a mode of life surpassing experience, not confirming it.

It is then only within a narrow historical range that categorical symbolism can be said to have been realized in works of art, namely, in those periods and among those people upon whom idealistic dogma and institutional religion had ceased to exert a decisive influence, but which had not yet adopted the modern willful deviation from representational practices. Both Rembrandt and Chardin can be cited as masters whose work lends itself to categorical expansion, because they are concerned with the humble, unassuming, and yet profoundly moving imperfections of individual things: Chardin with the modest world of food and household utensils and with the sacramental function which their service would bestow upon them if we were capable of sufficient gratitude; Rembrandt with the no less venerable quality of human beings which comes from the quietly devout acceptance of a lifetime of experience and from submission to whatever the future may hold in store. Both artists took their start from individual phenomena. Both refused to be absorbed in descriptive niceties, since their aim lay in evoking a general truth about the relation of the individual to the Deity.

While this truth is normally embodied in the work of art itself and thus accessible only to an intuitive approach, it is possible also to render it explicit by verbal analysis. Only great sensitivity, however, and a magisterial command of words will be able to do justice to this critical phase of categorical symbolism, which, although without prior knowledge of any class into which its objects may fit, must yet proceed from an intelligent appraisal and selection of their internal characteristics.

VIII *Legal Representation*

It is with some misgivings that we pass from
the discussion of categorical to that of legal and political representation, for we are here trespassing upon a
field that is autonomous in many ways and has evolved
its own specific terminology. To try to reproduce this
vocabulary here, and thus to interrupt the flow of our
argument, would be worse than useless. We shall continue to use the terms to which we have begun to grow
accustomed, replacing them by others from the legal
glossary only when these are so well known or so clearly
defined by the context in which they occur that even a
reader unprepared for legal argument will be able to
follow with ease.

What is it that happens when a man becomes a political representative and leaves his home to concern

himself at the capital with the interests and needs of the electorate?

I must first caution the reader that the preliminary steps that help to insure the fair execution of representative government are not to be confused with its functioning. The diverse methods of election designed to assure a distribution of power commensurate with the importance of various social and geographical groups—direct and indirect ballot, by district or on a national scale, a single body or a bicameral parliament—all these only serve to prepare future representational events. The same is true of the restrictions which different constitutions have placed on the nature of those eligible to vote or to to be voted into power. Arrangements such as these, important as they are in determining the nature of a parliamentary democracy, are as yet so far removed from the future political activity of the elected deputy that they cannot even bind his allegiance to the specific interests of his constituents; the conflict between loyalty to them and intelligent espousal of the general cause is one which every political representative must resolve for himself. To the detriment of the nation involved he often decides to sponsor the narrow local interest instead of devoting his time and strength to the greater issues at stake.

Still, the various electoral systems are not without interest from our point of view, since they express what may be called the substitutional side of parliamentary government. When a nation decides that it cannot govern itself by vote and popular referendum as do the Swiss in their direct democracy, then the question arises in what manner the unwieldy mass of the electorate is to be replaced by a more compact body of elected representatives. It will then be necessary to devise means through which the power originally vested in the population of voting age can be concentrated in a group of substitutes, who will be able to effect an easy interchange of views and thus to arrive at decisions more expeditiously than would a scattered electorate. All the various methods that statesmen have thought out for apportioning, channeling, and transferring political power are merely variants upon this central theme.

We have here another instance of a self-regulating system, except that the substitution that takes place in this case is an entirely internal one, requiring no rapacious forays into the outside world. The body politic may be regarded as the organism whose maintenance is to be assured, and the parliamentarian as an internal substitute appointed to see to its proper functioning, while the voters appear as determinants who initiate the process by exercising their constitutional rights. It is a confirmation for this view that in order to give validity to the results arrived at, they must be made binding upon those in whose name parliamentarians operate. Such preparation of legal enforcement is clearly not part of the representational process, which it often succeeds in the form of a vote or of the affixing of signatures to a document. But if it is true that political representation operates in the context of a larger framework, at the heart of a concentric process of self-determination, then the need to make its results obligatory is obvious. A parliament could not function as a collective substitute or (which is the same) as a central organ of the state, were it not able to compel the adherence of the citizenry to its decisions by giving to these the coercive quality of the law. Only thus can the substitutional methods of control of the body politic be truly effective.

There is, however, the essential difference between the parliamentary state and other substitutional systems that the voters, unlike other determinants, continue their interest in the activity of their deputies even after their power has been vested in them. In the usual systems, substitutes hold their places with such exclusive possessiveness that there can be no protracted supervision of their work by their determinants. In legal representation, on the contrary, the voters in a parliamentary state do not renounce their political rights when they put the fate of the ship of state in the hands of their chosen representatives. So far are they, in fact, from abdicating their prerogatives that they will often attempt to influence the decisions of the lawmakers through letters, lobbyists, and pressure groups, turning them out of office in due course if they fail to measure up to what was expected of them. There is, then, in legal and political representation a bifurcation of power that permits the continued active presence within the system of those who have delegated their political competence to their deputies.

It is justifiable to attribute this deviation from the usual pattern of substitution to the effect of representation itself, which compels the delegate to speak in the name of those who put their trust in him, and thus to conform as much as possible to their directives. If a parliamentary state were no more than a simple substitutional system, then the deputies, once installed, would find themselves without well-defined obligations toward their constituents. Reduced to consulting only their own insight, they would very soon perpetuate themselves in office as an autocratic clique, and end by disenfranchising their electorate.

Our first excursion into the field of political representation has thus netted us a rather important result, for we have seen that such representation is possible only within a substitutional system capable of providing it with a purpose. Whenever we ask what profit may be reaped from a representational arrangement, what needs it satisfies, and what improvements it supplies, we are asking about its substitutional function.

This is true not only of a deputy in relation to his electorate but of an appointed delegate as well; for we cannot conceive of the position of such a delegate without presupposing that he is a substitute at the same time: he cannot speak on his client's behalf without having first been put into the client's place. The very act of appointment to which he owes his prerogative has, beside its legal function, a substitutional one, since it is the means by which the future deputy is propelled into the arena of his political or legal activity. We find therefore that what holds of parliamentarians in a democracy holds equally, despite their rather different social functions, of attorneys, lawyers, vicars, and ambassadors, all of whom are appointed to act for and instead of their principals. Only their qualifications, that is, the reasons why they were chosen as substitutes, will differ from case to case.

Although representation is thus profoundly affected by its alliance with substitution, the latter undergoes significant changes of its own in consequence of its symbiosis with its sister function, for it loses its exclusiveness and begins to accommodate itself to the continued rights of the principal. Instead of superseding the entity for which it stands, the substitute is now open to the claims of that entity, with the result that both participants now coexist and remain in profitable contact. The delegate finds himself cast in a new role to which no mere substitute could be expected to adjust himself: he plays the intermediary between two opposing or contracting parties, for in addition to dealing with the interpretant before him, he remains under the continued control of his principal. He is thus faced with a delicate problem of double adjustment as he tries to accommodate his attitude to two conflicting claims and personalities. It is a legitimate part of the work of an attorney or ambassador to mediate, to smooth out difficulties, to overcome resentments, and thus to contribute to a better understanding between the governments and persons negotiating through him.

We have now acquainted ourselves with the substitutional aspects of political and legal representation, but we are still far from having attained an understanding of its structure. In order to accomplish this, it will be best to abandon our study of institutions and to concentrate upon the events which pass in the mind of the interpretant as he is faced with the bidden or unbidden presence of the delegate; since representation is a rational relation, we cannot come to grips with it unless we are ready to follow it into its mental stronghold.

But as we look upon it from the observer's vantage point, we must prepare ourselves for first meeting its substitutional aspect once more, and meeting it in its typically dynamic form; for it is inevitable that the deputy's relation to the system should be reflected in a corresponding attitude on the part of the interpretant. Whatever in the interpretant's dealings with the representative pertains to the conduct of negotiations—the disputing of points, the haggling over obligations or conditions, and the final agreement or compromise—still belongs to the world of substitution, only it is the interpretant this time who contributes his share to it. It is natural that he, no less than the principal of the opposing party, will have to bind himself to the compact by affixing his signature to it.

Legal representation is thus all-enveloped and permeated by substitution. It is not hard to understand why such representation should be styled as a formal event, with emphasis on status and mandate, for were it not for the maintenance of legal conventions there would be little to set it apart from more primitive forms of replacement. If the deputy could not prove his status it would be all too easy to mistake him for a substitute, and the cause he pleads for a venture without legal intention or validity.

Once more we may ask: What is legal representation? Let us assume that a lawyer or ambassador has called upon the opposing party and that the credentials, proof of his representational capacity, have been proffered and accepted. Let us assume, furthermore, that the interpretant is aware of the other party's identity but that he has no knowledge from any source of the business about to be transacted. We ask what will be his mental responses as he impresses upon himself the representational status of the person before him.

Two considerations will suggest themselves to him: he will be compelled to assume that there has been a mandate, an act of appointment, by virtue of which the person before him is entitled to act on behalf of his client; and he will assume that because of this mandate or because of conditions antecedent to it the deputy has agreed to regard the client's interest as his own.

Of these two automatic mental acts the first will be the condition of the second. We shall call it the rationale of representation, noting that this conferring of a quality upon a willing future delegate is an intransitive act which the principal directs toward the future deputy.

The alignment of the delegate's interest with that of his client (a no less indispensable factor in legal representation) is, by contrast, a transitive relation, and implies the belief on the part of the interpretant that the actions of the appointee will always be for the benefit of the principal and thus comparable to those which the principal would have performed had he chosen to take care of his own affairs. Drawing on our previous vocabulary we shall call this community of interest the basis of representation. The transfer of power, which is a formal act, and as such empty unless implemented, requires realization in the field of concrete political and legal relationships if it is to become operative. This realization, in turn, would lose its sanction if deprived of its rationale, resolving itself into a mere friendly and informal partnership. If there is to be an act of legal representation, both factors must complement each other, although both are autonomous by nature and possess their own fields of application: When a person is appointed to a job or when two people share their holdings and legal interests, no representation is implied.

It is possible, accordingly, that there will be a well-established community of business interest before the decision is taken to defend it by appointing one of its beneficiaries as a delegate; or that such an alignment will be artificially created, although there was no suggestion of it when the transfer of power took place. The first is the case of the spokesman who undertakes to vindicate the rights of his group because he belongs to it himself and thus acts out of enlightened self-interest. The second is that of the lawyer who, after having been given power of attorney, charges himself with the affairs of a client that had previously been alien and irrelevant to him. Even the appointment of an ambassador presupposes a genuine transfer of interests, for although he is likely to have been a member of his nation before he accepts his new task, and thus to have shared its prosperity and affliction, he now becomes a member of its government and thus obligates himself to take over its concrete and specific interests abroad. At any rate, the act of representation, if it is to benefit a human association, calls for a focusing of legal interests, preparatory to entrusting them to the appointed delegate. These interests have been the common possession of the members of the group. Now they are gathered into a single compact entity, so that the delegate may charge himself with it when he gets ready to enter into the active phase of his career.

We now owe the reader an explanation of why we have chosen to call the appointment of the legal representative the rationale of representation, implying in the choice of that term that whatever the event contains of self-evident truth resides, in part at least, in this initial step. There is, if you will, a gradation of increasing evidential accuracy as we ascend from the surface of representation, its area of contact with the outer world, toward its focal area. What evidence there is in the communicative aspect of representation, in the information it conveys, is of course inaccurate, since what the delegate chooses to disclose is filtered through the sieve of his personality and given diversity by the discretion he may possess of varying his message within a certain latitude. Even assuming that he is careful not to exceed his mandate, he may present the interpretant with a very personal and hence possibly one-sided version of the truth. We come closer to the phenomenon of rationality when we consider the alignment or community of interest, which helps to assure the truth of what is said, for this relation is accessible only to intellectual intuition, and as such has no factual existence, as long at least as no specific revelations have been made about the intentions of the principal.

It is, however, only when considering the appointment of the delegate and the convictions of the interpretant about it that we enter into the area of true self-evidence, for the very act by which the representative introduces himself as such entails implications that the interpretant will have to regard as necessary and inevitable. As he faces the delegate, the observer will be compelled to realize that the person before him is the one chosen among an indefinite number of candidates whose appointment would have been equally possible; and he will be aware also that although the candidates could have been many, the principal was only one, for no more than one client can be served in the course of one single representational act. When the individuals represented are many, as in the case of the constituency of a political delegate, they must be conceived, from the interpretant's point of view, as one large and undifferentiated group.

We find thus that the relation of a client to his possible representatives, like that of the whole to its parts, rests upon the contrast between one single entity and its potential dependents, except that what in categorical representation consists of the internal subdivision of a totality, now becomes an external dominance of a person (or group) over others devoted to his cause. In both cases the uniqueness of the principal is assured, while the number and character of its dependents remains a matter of surmise. It is always possible that more than one delegate will be retained to occupy them-

selves with various phases of business or to negotiate
with several interpretants: witness the fact that nothing less than a whole diplomatic corps will suffice to represent a government at various foreign capitals. Where
there is only one active representative, the others who
might have been employed remain present in the mind
of the interpretant as potential alternatives, regardless
of the facts of the case. Even if we happen to know that
a person living in a deserted or sparsely settled region
has only one lawyer available who can defend him in
court, this limitation in the world of fact does not mili-
tate against our imputing to him an ideal choice unaffected by circumstances. Such liberty is independent of
the conditions under which real decisions are made.

This, then, is the heart of the matter: We find that
representation rests upon the principle of choice, which
is an exercise of freedom on the part of the principal,
and therefore springs from the very concept of the human personality. Since it does, and since the relation of
the two concepts is inevitable, we have here the element
of self-evidence which we are seeking. Just as the very
idea of a whole involves the existence of parts, so does
that of the human personality imply that of the autonomy of choice.

But while the rationale of categorical representation
is simple, its legal counterpart has a double nature; the
choice involved in it is twofold, comprising (1) a natural event, such as occurs whenever a person embarks on
a course of action, and in intimate union with it (2) a
purely formal one that endows this action with its legal
quality. While both of these aspects of freedom form
part of the assumption by the interpretant that an appointment has taken place, it is the legal aspect alone
that makes of it the beginning of a representational

event, for that event is a transfer of interest, i.e., a formal act. It settles upon the deputy a secondary legal quality, enabling him to behave as if he were the principal and thus endowing his decisions with the same double quality, natural and legal, which his client was the first to possess. Unless the appointment has been given legal character, the interpretant will be free to hold that the actions of the deputy are merely informal communications, valuable perhaps for an intelligent appraisal of opinions held on the other side but without legal consequence.

It will be understood, on the other hand, that since representation as here described consists of the union of a natural and of a legal event, riveted together by the free will of the principal, there may be conditions under which their co-operation will cease. When a political delegate responds to the need of his nation rather than to that of the group of constituents who voted him into power, or when a lawyer appointed by a guardian performs his duty toward the child whose affairs he is to take to heart, then the representational relation splits wide open. It divides into the natural and dynamic function which propels the delegate into the field of his future activity, and into the formal one that justifies his action, the latter by now only a fiction, since the act of appointment has not been performed by the person or group represented.

We have dealt so far with those a priori categories which the interpretant will apply once he has been advised that an act of representation is about to take place, categories which provide a rational framework for any concrete event than can be fitted into them. As yet there is no awareness on the part of the interpretant of what the deputy will reveal to him, except for a general expectation that it will pertain to the party named. There is no knowledge as yet about the concrete interests at stake and thus about the individual identity of the principal, who cannot be completely defined in legal terms except by virtue of the rights, claims, and immunities which cluster about him. The name of the person represented is as yet a mere label attached to an undefined particular.

It is worthwhile to stop here for a moment in order to take stock of the situation described, for it is possible to arrest the representational process at the point where we have now arrived, without allowing it to proceed to the concrete particulars which the later activities by the deputy will inject into it. The result is curious and instructive: representation, at this stage, is as vague as it is comprehensive, a mere matter of conviction to be impressed upon the waiting interpretant. Since it is as yet without articulate content that could become the subject of bargaining between the parties concerned, the interpretant cannot take that active attitude which he would assume if he were confronted with specific business. Having gone through the initial rational considerations which the situation demands, he finds himself reduced to merely accepting whatever the appearance before him of the delegate may have in store: an implicit expectation which the delegate will want to honor or possibly exploit by increasing the outer paraphernalia of his status and manifesting them for all to see by a display of pageantry.

It is, in short, the preliminary and comprehensive phase of representation that expresses itself through pomp and circumstance or, if these are lacking, through the proud and self-confident pose of the delegate. Just as categorical representation, if arrested, turns from a scientific into an aesthetic phenomenon, so does political representation begin to address our sensations and sensibilities, if it is prevented from discharging its practical potential. The reasons are the same: since there is to be no interaction between the representative and the interpretant, the latter is deprived of his chance of ascertaining the intentions of his visitor by entering into negotiations with him. If he has no means of testing the inexplicable presence of the delegate for its concrete and tangible motivation, he can regard it only as a sensuous phenomenon. And the delegate, who is forced to establish his representational capacity without recourse to a specific agenda, is very naturally led to bolstering his status by a display of synthetic grandeur.

It is not, however, only the desire to impress that will prompt the representative to load himself with glamorous ornaments, for his own status is intrinsically altered when there is little immediate prospect of implementing the preliminary moves by getting down to business. If the representational process arrives at a premature halt, before having been focused upon practical concerns, then the categories upon which it rests cease to remain a mere framework and take on the character of lasting and material substances. The act of appointment becomes one of bestowing a permanent quality upon the delegate, an undefined aura that will detach itself from its source and settle upon its newly chosen recipient. Although, when practical concerns are uppermost, the transfer of power will find vent in representational action, and thus not affect the person of the delegate, this conferring of a magical potency leaves him intrinsically altered, a chosen vessel for essences foreign to his nature. The community of interests will seem more like a union of undefinable but very real potencies than it will like a necessary hypothesis for a transaction within the law. What would have been a formal assignment, if it had been allowed to run its course, will thus receive the character of a consecration, with its attendant transfer of power by symbolic means. The representational act itself, incapable of revealing anything new, will tend to assume a stringent ceremonial pattern and to impose this pattern upon repeat performances until a complete identity of ritual actions is attained.

Neither the anointing of the king nor the appointment of the lawyer would be possible, however, if the human personality itself were not so profoundly involved in all representational action. Unlike substitutes, whose obligations exhaust themselves in conceding to their systems what they want and no more, the legal representative is called upon to give himself entirely and without stint when he becomes a delegate, for he enters his task not as a member of a species possessing certain useful traits but as an individual. He is expected to draw upon his resources of personality and training and to project himself into the role which his task imposes upon him. Even those of his faculties which do not enter into his present business are to be available for service when they are wanted.

Assume now that the preliminary phase of representation is over and that the delegate launches into his specific task. His initiative will cause an immediate reorientation on the part of the interpretant from formal or magic considerations to realities. His indeterminate expectation will give way to a gradual acknowledgment of the facts in the case, his intuitive attitude to a readiness to take an active hand in negotiations. Instead of conceiving of the principal as a mere focus of undefined formal interests, he will now learn to see in him a concrete individual engaged in some particular business.

Both the representative and his client may thus lose stature as their presumptive rights are cut down to the size of their true affairs, but they will also gain in distinctness and substance. We must maintain, at any rate, that no particular case which representation may put forward can exhaust the wealth of legal potentialities clustering about the person of the principal, since not even an indefinite number of representational acts performed in varying contingencies could hope to exhaust it. Each concrete case of representation thus exhibits only a mere facet of a total legal existence and therefore entails a contrast between the unique entity denoted and the multiple aspects through which it can be viewed.

As representation becomes a tool for concrete legal transactions, the categories in terms of which the interpretant views it will not cease to operate. They continue as a permanent rational framework within which the actual process of representation is to unfold, only they cease to hold our attention once representation has been refocused upon specific issues. Since these categories are no more than a priori presuppositions which precede any kind of representational event, they contain in themselves neither limitations nor restrictions upon the kind of relation they will enclose, except for a general condition that whatever the delegate decides to undertake must not be against the interest of the principal. The question of what constitutes such interest is to be decided by the latter or by the two together in a preliminary conference.

The control of what the delegate's message may

transmit is thus not an a priori implication of representation, and must be undertaken expressly. The mandate given by the client must be supplemented by detailed directives stating in what business the delegate may engage, and how far he may go in pursuing it. The deputy in turn will have to impose definite obligations upon himself if he is to do justice to his task, undertaking to keep himself within the limits of his directives, to offer a full and adequate presentation of the case, and to avoid the pitfalls of superfluity and irrelevance. No formal criterion of his representational status will protect him against the demands of adequacy, which operate in the world of fact, and against the annulment of his privilege, which is likely to ensue if he fails.

Finally, a word should be said about the attitude of the interpretant as he finds himself faced with the specific message of the delegate, for it will be his task to check upon the truth of what has been said to him, not only by applying the internal criteria of plausibility and consistency but also, if necessary, by direct recourse to the principal. It is not likely, however, that he will want to engage in investigations of this kind unless the deputy has been unconvincing, untruthful, or clumsy in the presentation of his case. If the deputy is successful, using his personality as a vehicle for the statement of a trustworthy cause, the fascination of his presence will tend to make the interpretant dismiss all thought of the principal for the time being. As always when it is really operative, representation will become a surface phenomenon, and thus will paradoxically reduce the person in whose name it is undertaken to the status of an annex or of an ephemeral afterthought.

IX *Mimetic Representation*

A definite design has begun to delineate itself. As we look back upon the results of the last two chapters, we cannot fail to notice how every element of structure which we discovered in categorical representation made its appearance once more during our analysis of its legal counterpart, although their obvious similarity is modified by the need of fitting each into its own divergent pattern of experience. The parallelism is complete and convincing, based as it is on the following points of coincidence: the presence in both legal and categorical representation of a twofold rational framework consisting of a transitive and an intransitive factor; their dominance during a first arrested and symbolic phase and their persistence into a second and active one; the slow and always incomplete disclosure of the true nature of the principal; the latitude accorded to the representamen in performing its expository function; the tendency on the part of the interpretant to be lulled into acceptance of a possibly unreliable message; finally the fact that in its own distinctive way each type of representation is imbedded in and supported by substitution. There is enough here that is unvarying and uniform to encourage the belief that we have indeed found the fundamentals of representation which underlie and transcend their application in particular legal and logical contexts.

We turn now, with this expectation in mind, to the last of the basic types of representation, which we shall call mimetic, since it embodies the vast field of intelligence through imitation, i.e., of representational pictures or sculptures, of performances, descriptions, narrations, notations, maps, graphs, and diagrams, an enormously widespread and varied group comprising a large part of all human artifacts and activities. Our results to date encourage us to believe that these, too, despite their prodigious multiplicity, share certain simple rational presuppositions.

We have no difficulty in isolating the common basis of mimetic representation, which is the principle of resemblance, for all the objects enumerated are likenesses which represent by virtue of similarity, natural or conventional. The principle thus postulated has all the characteristics found in common essence and community of interest, for resemblance, like its sister function, is a reciprocal and concrete relation which has its own field of application prior to any effort to engage its help in the establishment of a representational state.

We find the rationale of mimetic representation in the relation of its subject to the various realizations in foreign media of which it is capable: the relation of a mythological scene to the pictures that could be painted of it, of a play to the performances through which it may be brought to life, of a real or imaginary event to the narratives which may be devoted to its recitation. Once more, as in the cases previously analyzed, we have the necessary opposition of a single principal to its potential multiple dependents, for it is the nature of subjects—any subjects—that they are capable of, and in a sense in need of, expansion through their incarnation in foreign substances. Therefore, if an interpretant is confronted with a likeness, unless he is entirely immersed in it, he will realize that what he beholds is only one among an indefinite number of other likenesses that could be made of this one theme if the desire prevailed. The subject, if he is aware of it at all, will appear to him as if it were surrounded by an array of reflections in a mirror cabinet.

We notice once more, as we did previously, how well the rationale and the basis of representation supplement each other, for resemblance, taken singly, would be indiscriminate and uncontrolled, while the principle of embodiment would be empty if its more concrete sister function did not make up for its native deficiency. Only when both co-operate does representation come to pass, consolidating itself through the recognition of its two component parts in one rapid, almost instantaneous mental act. As in categorical and legal representation the rationale has the logical priority, for while it is possible to notice resemblance without inferring that a likeness is at hand, it is not possible to recognize a realization, say, in one of the media of the visual arts, without the immediate knowledge that what we see is meant to represent. It is thus the interpretant's task when confronted with likenesses of any kind to contribute a rational framework of his own, by means of which their message may be grasped, and to do so irrespective of whether he has had a chance to learn what real subject the artist had in mind. It is his privilege to construct his own version of what the likeness intends to convey.

The real subject, on the other hand, whose identity he may or may not correctly surmise, corresponds to the reality beyond the interpretant's world whose existence we noted in commenting upon representation in its categorical and legal phase. For it belongs to that store of assumptions, ideas, and interests to which the artist had access, and thus has a mode of existence which transcends the interpretant's world. Its life lies upon the intellectual plane, and its validity is due to its being a point of contact between an objective possibility and the interests of a cultural community. Even when it can be immediately grasped—such as the subject of a landscape or of cows in a pasture—it always has its life among things whose existence does not depend upon the mode of thought which the interpretant brings to the understanding of it. Thus his task is to reach beyond the region which his categories unlock and to seek realities, engaging, if need be, in iconographic research to determine the representational intent that guided the artist's hand. It must be added, in order to show the parallelism with other representational types, that the rational framework will remain intact through all the changes of thought that such a new orientation may compel, simply because without it representation would collapse.

What we may call the freedom of artistic likenesses, comparable to the latitude of lawyers and specimens, results from the determinant's assurance that his work, once elementary recognition is obtained, will be spontaneously received as representational. Whatever he decides to represent, and no matter what aspects he may select, he can always rely upon our willingness to believe—unless proof to the contrary has been gained —that the realization of a subject is at hand. Likenesses have an intensive and qualitative diversity, not only a numerical and extensive one, and thus assert once more their kinship with other representational types. No rendering, however penetrating and accurate, will ever exhaust the inner wealth of its subject, since it is the nature of likenesses to be limited to a given slant and to contingent and fragmentary aspects. Just as the full inner richness of a species or of the sum total of a person's legal affairs transcends all the approaches to them that can be devised, so the subject as a source of invention surpasses all possible realizations.

That mimetic representation has a primary and arrested phase, during which its perceptible qualities prevail over whatever information it may relay, must be evident to a reader who has ever stood before a picture, entranced with the way its surface organization was interwoven with its representational capacity. He will remember that, as his aesthetic pleasure deepened, he abandoned all thought of a subject capable of being given substance in other pictures, for what he experienced was concentrated within the visible entity before him. To the truly rapt spectator there is no such thing as resemblance to a subject or a choice of materials, since the painting has a glorious presence that radiates its own message. He sees it as a primary phenomenon free from background entanglements, which reveals its secret in contemplation only, not to the active attitudes of historical and iconographic inquiry. Thus for him the rational framework ceases to point to a "meaning," its relational capacity dwindles, and it becomes one with the fabric of the painting. As always when the interpretant ceases to be active, the representamen absorbs its matrix, having used it as a mould in which to distill its own charged reality.

We shall end this short review of the resemblances between mimetic and the other forms of representation by pointing to its close alliance with processes of substitution. A picture or sculpture contemplated for its own sake will always be able to do without the support of vicarious functions. But shift your interest from its surface to its subject, from enjoyment to the exploitation of its utility, and a significant reorientation will take place. It will then be found that the likeness serves the satisfaction of an interest or drive and that the latter demands a short cut to experience because its object is too remote, complex, or disjointed to be approached directly. A map, which represents a region, may also replace a vague spatial notion by a concrete and measurable image; the perusal of a score that represents a symphony may substitute for its performance, precisely because the attentive reader will be thinking of the real music; or, finally, to the worshiper a painting of the Virgin Mary may stand for—that is be substituted for—her presence. It is always possible, in other words, to insert an element of vicariousness into mimetic representation, provided that the subject be regarded as real and that an active attitude be adopted toward it. It is true also that, although relations between lawyers and clients or between samples and their classes are never without the ingredient of substitution, likenesses may be regarded in this light only if the circumstances permit.

Thus (although short and necessarily superficial) our first survey has shown that likenesses have the same inner structure as other representamina and that our field of inquiry is essentially one. We can now proceed to the further argument that the three basic types of representation—categorical, legal, and mimetic—are the only ones that can and do exist; and to the implication, which we shall not yet elaborate, that all other representamina—e.g., symbolic and allegorical—must either be derived from one of these three or be phases in their logical development. The reason lies in the limitations which the nature of things imposes upon the relation between representamina and their principals. That relation can be an internal one, as in the case of specimens and samples, which are always enclosed by and thus part of their class; they are the simplest and most artless of representations and the easiest to understand. It can be external, in the case of lawyers and political representatives, independent beings who, apart from their legal work, owe no logical or metaphysical debt to their principals. It stands to reason that their representational capacity, which nature, unaided, hardly abetted or prepared, must be outwardly conferred upon them; and that their relation to their principals is thus an artificial and fictitious one grafted upon substitution. Finally there are the likenesses, whose connection with their subject is neither external nor internal, since they only reflect what they render, instead of being contained by it or accommodating themselves to its extraneous and formal demands. While never of the same class as the subject they portray—the medium sees to that—they allude to it through powerful analogies, and thus remain close to their subject while at the same time dissociating themselves from it. They are at once intimately allied with and aloof from their principals. It is evident that their analogical status, with its fusion of external and internal relationships, is the only one that remains after the two other modes have been defined, and that we have thus exhausted the gamut of ontological possibilities.

Thus the position of likenesses is a singular one, which lifts them beyond the monotony of logical fact and the formality of legal utterance. They are the only representamina whose being is almost always identical with their representational capacity, embodied as they are in foreign substances. They are mere daubs or senseless sounds unless they engage in their representational task. It is thus their very nature to represent, whereas samples are objects and attorneys are men whether or not they accommodate themselves to a representational role.

The consequences become apparent as soon as the various types are examined in their arrested phases, when they rely upon the effect of their *mise en scène* rather than upon our awareness of complex background relationships. We saw that at that stage both categorical and legal representatives refuse to relay a specific message, preferring, if the matter can be put that way, to be accepted "en bloc"; and that both proffer themselves, in their various ways, charged with an indeterminate quality, which clusters around them like a halo instead of adhering to any particular part. At that early stage the precise nature of the principal is not known. There can be no question, therefore, of focusing upon selected attributes and activities, since each of these is a point of contact with a species or a group of legal interests and thus leads us to a dimension beyond. The phase of symbolic awareness is thus bound to end at the very moment when the revelation of particulars begins, which launches samples and lawyers alike upon the active phases of their representational careers.

This is not so in the case of likenesses, for their representational capacity is never laid aside, not even when they linger in their arrested phase, which their sister functions exploit to indulge in symbolic ambiguities. Even then every part of a likeness retains its representational function and thus contributes to the intensive character of the whole. Instead of dwelling in a cloud of indistinct but pervasive significance, likenesses are thus accustomed to rely upon details as vehicles of their representational life. They can be examined and enjoyed without compelling their admirers to pass from contemplation to more active attitudes that will promote contact with the region of prototypes.

The results of this conclusion are far-reaching. For if it is true that likenesses formulate their message before the encounter with their subjects takes place, then it must be said that, in a sense unknown to other representational types, likenesses are free from the usual dependence upon principals. We must then accept the paradox that their status, which marks them as indirect and derivative, confers upon them at the same time the strength required to make them hold their own against their prototypes. Or to speak in more concrete terms: pictures, sculptures, and narratives carry their own import as representamina, an import which adheres to them irrespective of the nature of their principals. This content, which their very presence implies, is an independent, logical function and therefore accessible to us even though we may be ignorant of what the artist really had in mind. It allows us thus to establish a presumed subject of our own on the basis of the evidence before us, without attempting to ascertain what the real topic may have been. Both may, but need not, coincide. To speak of representation and its subject matter as if they were interchangeable terms (an abuse of language common even among distinguished iconographers) is not permissible.

We shall finish this chapter by returning once more to the difference between the three chief kinds of representation, in order to find out this time how it affects the relation between the determinant and the other participants in the common enterprise. It is the determinant's task to release the train of events. He will therefore have to fit himself in wherever his work as a generator is demanded by the other representational parts. When relating classes and specimens he will thus be one with the interpretant, for his business will be merely to observe, not to create, as a witness to a pre-existing natural fact. His only way of interfering with the course of events will be to choose the sample or group of samples upon which he himself will train his analytic intelligence.

The legal determinant, in contrast, has his being on the far side of the representational scheme, for the pre-existing relation is now one between the principal and the interpretant, and the determinant's task is that of a delegate between them. No wonder that substitution plays a more decisive role here than it does in the other types of representation. Since the interpretant, on his side, expects the delegate to arrive loaded with interests conferred upon him through the care and action of the determinant, he cannot himself attempt a similar role and try to undertake the choice of a middleman. If he does he will merely have appointed a second delegate who will confront his legal opposite and conduct negotiations with him to the exclusion of both principals.

Likenesses, finally, impart upon the determinant the privilege of dealing with representation on its own plane, that is, neither from the vantage point of the interpretant nor of the principal, freeing him thus from the pressure of representational events. Instead of reshuffling entities to whose existence he could not have contributed, he is thus given the opportunity to create, since neither principal nor interpretant can interfere with his productive activity. Alone among various types of determinants he has a chance to give to the material at hand his own imaginative cast.

X   *The Rationale*
of Mimetic Representation

We hope to have suggested by now why likenesses, in spite of their kinship with other representational types, surpass them all in terms of variety and versatility. It will now be our task to traverse once more the territory through which we have passed and to examine at leisure and in greater detail the stages in our reasoning. We shall sharpen our tools and use them to approach the nature of the rationale.

It has been claimed that mimetic representation comes to pass because the interpretant is aware that the picture, sculpture, or narrative, whichever he may happen to behold, embodies only one among many possible realizations of the subject. The attentive reader will have observed that we have fallen short of proving the main point in our argument: i.e., the contention that this relation of a likeness to its theme and to all other possible realizations of it is indeed a necessary and rational one in the sense that it is implied by the very nature of its component parts.

In order to supply this proof it may be useful to remind ourselves once more of what we mean when we speak of a likeness. We suggest that it is a representation so disposed that the manner in which its materials are arranged reflects some aspect or projection of its subject. The emphasis in this definition lies upon the two limiting terms, for likenesses, so we must insist, are always partial and incomplete and thus fundamentally different from duplicates and replicas. Any theory that sees the artist's task as that of counterfeiting reality rather than expounding and translating it must thus be emphatically denied.

As soon, however, as duplicates and replicas are out of the way, the rationale of representation becomes manifest; for it is then clear that the very existence of a likeness implies that there might be others differently conceived and viewed from different vantage points but reproducing the same theme, although none of them would be able to compete with the plenitude of the theme. Thus when a topic in the visual arts has a certain extension in time and space, it will suffice to curtail its dimensions, to compress it, as it were, into a narrower scope, to create by implication a bundle of other likenesses which will be potential realizations of the same theme. That this is indeed a rational relation is evident, for we cannot think of an aspect or a method of description without implying in the mental act that there are others equally valid, even though nobody may as yet have set himself the task of bringing them to light; in this matter, there is a complete harmony between the nature of things and the inclination of the human mind.

Thus in creating a likeness it is imperative to avoid too close an approximation of reality while attempting, at the same time, to render it in convincing terms: a paradoxical set of demands which has determined the artist's task, stimulating him yet limiting his scope, throughout the long history of his endeavors. His freedom of creation will be very great as long as the medium is remote from the things expressed, permitting the literary man, because of the abstractness of his medium, to depict anything that falls under his purview. The sculptor, on the other hand, whose work lies within three-dimensional space, has to submit to greater restraint, for he is beset by the risk of duplicating things instead of representing them. He cannot afford to make a likeness of such things as a stone or an egg, no more than of a landscape or of a house, for if he does he will merely produce a replica or a small-scale model of his theme, disqualifying himself as an artist. He will, we may say, have competed ineffectually with nature. His legitimate field of interest lies among organic entities whose spontaneous movement provides them with a dimension in excess of those which his inert creation can possess. He will be wise to limit his work to the representation of animals and men, adding, when his task demands, loose garments reflecting the human shape and, at the most, some identifying attributes. He will have reached and perhaps transcended the boundaries of his art if he places architectural structures and landscape in the background of pictorial reliefs. Painting, by contrast, has the entire visible world for its domain, as a reward for lacking the dimensions of both time and depth.

Even when the various arts observe the restraints which their materials put upon them, there is still the risk that the artist's work may seem to impinge upon the everyday world and thus present itself, against his wish, as a deceptive substitute. He must then guard his work against being misunderstood, and he does so by various devices that lift it out of the context of practical concerns. Frames, the bases of statues, and the theatrical proscenium are such tools, contrived in order to surround the work of art with a layer of protective insulation and thus to insure it against the danger of being mistaken for reality itself. They help to inform the interpretant that what he sees is a stranger to his world, not to be treated as if it were of the same kind as the common run of things; and they suggest to him appropriate attitudes, receptive and contemplative, which will enable him to forget his usual pursuits, to concentrate upon the work of art, and to open himself to its impact. Thus a performance in the theater could easily be mistaken for part of real life, leading the spectators to interfere, if the very setting in which it takes place and its separation from the auditorium did not proclaim the illusory character of the action.

We would like to add, since it is often overlooked, that the rule of exclusion holds even here, in spite of what appears to be a very close approximation to reality: instead of the continuum of time and space in which our life unfolds, with its incessant shift of scene, we now face a stationary frame of action. The stabilization of space, in turn, implies that time will also be manipulated and condensed to adjust it to the requirements of the stage. It will be necessary to show either a narrow sector of events, in order to preserve the unity of space, or to cut its continuous flow into sepa-

rate scenes. Where the attempt is made to present interlocking incidents in their variety and epic breadth—a
task more congenial to the cinema than it is to the stage
—it will be necessary to resort to cutbacks and other
sudden changes of time and space. Thus when applied
to the theatrical arts, the partial aspect, which we attributed to likenesses of all kinds, extends to the dimensions of both space and time, implying that each must
be curtailed and reshaped and their relation redefined
if the level of art is to be reached.

Mimetic representation, so we must conclude, owes
its life to a prohibition, which protects it against abuse
by insisting that its analogical sense must not be allowed
to degenerate into a semblance of identity. There is more
than a superficial similarity—and we anticipate as we
speak of this—between this injunction and the other
one, well known from the Old Testament, that no direct
image of any kind is to be made of the Deity. For in the
field of religious thought the likeness itself is treated as
a replica, with the attendant implications of identity, so
that only the symbol, with its indirect and oblique mode
of reference, can be regarded as analogical. With the
immediate path toward reality closed by the command
either of piety or of good taste, man is compelled to
seek a less ambitious approach.

But, the reader may interpose, the prohibition
against replicas has often been flouted or overlooked
without drawing upon the artist's head the reproach
that his product has ceased to be representational. This
observation is true enough, since there are waxworks,
sculptures designed without pedestal, and models of
landscapes, houses, and machines, all of which our
theory roundly condemns while popular usage stamps
them as representational. To explain this discrepancy

we must avail ourselves of a rule which provides the link between legitimate and illegitimate representational types: namely, that for the interpretant evidence of the will to represent outweighs any ineptness or wrong-headedness in carrying it out. That is why dummies and waxworks are so perplexing to behold after the first deceptions have been cleared away, since we cannot help being scandalized by them, while we are at the same time compelled to acknowledge their representational claims.

About the universality of the rule there can be no doubt, for any artifact with a semblance imprinted on it will make the beholder conclude that it has been produced with an intention to represent. He will assume that the likeness has been made in order to convey a content to an audience, although the artist could not have foreseen its size and historical extent. Finding himself addressed and obliged to respond, the interpretant will attempt to grasp the meaning of the intelligence at hand. Ineptness in carrying out a representational aim will not diminish the beholder's readiness to receive; in fact, the beholder will be more strongly—and perhaps painfully—aware of an intention to represent if the artist has not fully achieved his goal. The gap that may exist between sensuous fact and representational aim will be closed only when the artist succeeds in expressing what he wanted to say or, which is almost the same, in creating a work of art.

The law of the supremacy of representational intent, as we shall call it, thus follows from another rule of ours, i.e., that likenesses carry the evidence of their function in themselves, and must therefore be read as testimonials to their own purpose. Only rarely does it happen that the intention to represent is announced in advance—in the manner of the lawyer presenting his brief—as when a storyteller leans back in his chair and declares that he is going to spin a yarn. It may be necessary at times to append an explanatory note to the likeness so as to establish its character in the interpretant's mind, if its appearance is so abstract (e.g., in the case of graphs and diagrams) that it will not explain itself.

The inner circle of legitimate representamina is thus surrounded by an outer one of those that fail to live up to minimum logical demands, either because the claims of the rationale are not recognized—as in the case of models, dummies, and effigies—or because their maker has failed to make the semblance sufficiently complete. Some of them overshoot the mark and land, as it were, in the field of primary reality, while others do not even manage to attain full status as representamina.

The likenesses that do not reach full status include descriptive gestures, those "drawings in the air" whose fleeting, imaginary lines are meant to convey a size, a shape, or the character of a dramatic event. Nobody will want to deny that these are representational in intent, particularly since they are likely to receive support from accompanying words. But it will also be agreed that they are too evanescent to bear out their claim and that they remain below the threshold of a full representational state. A man who acts a part without benefit of a stage will be in a similar predicament, even though he may employ all the resources of his art in imitating another person's idiosyncracies. That his behavior is representational at all will be recognized only if he succeeds in convincing others that his pose is a playful one, assumed in order to instruct or to divert. If he takes on his mask merely in order to hide under a protective new identity—the case of the spy or of the fugitive—or because his character is too weak to state itself in its own terms, then his behavior will be regarded as either natural or the result of pretense and explained without reference to representational purposes. In any event, the full status of representation cannot be reached in this way, since the actor's art demands the background and complement of a stage. His gestures require, as we shall later explain, a field of spatial reference if they are to be received into the representational domain.

It is because he assumes awareness of an intention to represent that the artist can play tricks with our state of mind by operating close—some would say, perilously close—to the boundary between his and the real world. If he is a painter, he may place the figures so far forward in space that they will seem to disport themselves in front of the frame. And if the theater is his field, he may try the even more audacious trick of having the action begin within the audience itself or of carrying it there from the stage: devices which, although they may at first confuse and disconcert, usually resolve themselves into aesthetic delight. The reason why such experiments, daring as they are, do not seem to fall beyond the pale of art, lies in the fact that we remain residually aware of representational intent while trying to cope with encroachments upon the real world. We know, even at the moment of the greatest surprise, that there is a stage or a picture plane, and thus are able, with a modicum of good will, to think of the rest as an extension forward of the representational scheme. The case is somewhat similar to that of direct speech imbedded within a narrative, such as exclamations, questions, and commands, which are not representational in themselves but may receive that quality from the context in which they appear. Illusionistic tricks are thus legitimate, as long as they occur within the environment of a work of art, enabling us to relate projecting and seemingly real parts to a representational core. Only if the situation is changed from an artistic to a practical one does illusionism show its evil side.

The presence of an appropriate intent is thus the minimum requirement without which no object or event can represent, not even illegitimately, so that the non-purposive fields of nature and of chance are excluded from the application of the term. No matter how much an oddly-shaped spot on the wall may be fraught with imagery, evoking the outlines of animals, battle scenes, or of human physiognomy, they do not represent, since they are the work of accident and thus beyond the reach of conscious intent. It makes no difference, in this respect, that they fulfill our primary logical demands by embodying the semblance of things in a foreign medium. Even if a chance event is the result of human activity, as are the ink spots of the Rorschach test, the level of representation is not attained, and the beholder is within his rights when he interprets the event according to his whim or to the promptings of his psychic state. If they are to reach the representational stage, such accidental lineaments must be reshaped, so that their artificial form, now rendered unambiguous, may bear testimony to human aims. It will then be possible to stabilize that which had been previously subjective and indeterminate, and to open it to the view and enjoyment of all.

The process of reshaping chance images seems to have played a very major part in the origin of the visual arts, since it helped to bridge the gap between inner imagery and a public portrayal in stone or in paint. The record is written in the ceilings of French and Spanish caves, where the artists of the post-glacial age depicted the bygone fauna of their day. They often placed their images so that irregularities in the stone, such as projections and minor fissures, would coincide with the outline of the animals portrayed. Creation seems to have begun when the artist found himself faced with the semblance of an animal immobilized far from its normal haunts, because of his own ability to project his imagery upon surfaces. He then redrew and emphasized the outline of what he saw, assured that the stone itself and its casual shape would hold the image in place, and ended, once he possessed the necessary technique, by filling in the missing parts in black and in red. A similar interpretation of the work of chance, this time of the scribbles caused by his own motor activity, inaugurates the phase of representational art in the development of the very young child.

It is obvious, at any rate, that in order to play its public role and to communicate ideas and shapes, representation must avail itself of a medium, as the only means by which it can make itself manifest, for what we called the intention to represent will not be able to come to the fore unless the likeness acquires substance and strength through some material embodiment. Once more we find a large group of phenomena approaching a full-blown representational state without being able to pass across its invisible frontiers, since mental images, if sufficiently vivid and permanent, are closely akin to likenesses but without their clear-cut existence in space and their definite materiality. It is by no means surprising to find that when man acquires the skill of controlling his imaginings, there is a fluid transition between the latter and visual art. Thus the tantric mystic of India may teach himself, through the concentrated effort of months and years, to conceive the traditional image of a deity down to minute details, to conjure it up at will and to project it in his devotions upon a lump of clay. The precision of his psychic workmanship may be quite the equal of that which others bestow upon idols of bronze and gold, so that it is only a step from the product of his mental activity to representational art. Yet we must maintain that this step is the decisive one and that the mystic, while evoking or conjuring up the god in his sensuous hypostasis, fails to represent him in the proper sense.

Once the logical requirements of representation are discharged, the interpretant finds himself confronted with what he now has the right to regard as a full-fledged embodiment of its theme. It is astonishing how quickly he goes through the preliminary mental acts, provided that there are no obstacles in the way, and proceeds to orient himself in the world to which the likeness belongs. Awareness both of the rationale and of resemblance fade away and instead there is a simple sense of a phenomenon in which the components of representation are no longer experienced as such. We speak of a landscape, a still life, a Madonna, without asking ourselves how we arrived at bestowing such names upon artifacts, because we have classified them as types once their representational function was confirmed. Thus all those distinctions through which the mind may have passed—between the subject and its import and between both and the material in which they have been cast—are forgotten before the newly-acquired sense of the likeness as a member of a realm possessing its own order and its own assortment of types.

But classification is only a preliminary step, to be

left behind as soon as orientation is complete and the interpretant is finally faced with the situation for which the majority of likenesses are made: namely, with the awareness of the unique claim which a particular work of art makes upon him. We ask ourselves what happens to the framework of representation as the interpretant's mind begins to concentrate upon the likeness at hand and to submerge itself in a contemplative state.

At that moment a new law comes into play, a correlate of that which postulates the potential plurality of representamina. It states that any likeness unites with that which it represents whenever we experience it as the only means by which its referent can be conveyed. Or conversely: a subject will maintain itself as distinct and separate only when the beholder is aware of the existence of various ways, even though none be specifically known, in which its content may be expressed. In the latter form the rule is familiar to us as the injunction of every good teacher, that we must never state a subject in the exact terms in which we have learned it, lest the method of description replace that which it is meant to describe. For only if we are aware that our modes of knowledge are variable and relative can we hope to come to grips with the reality to which they apply. The principle holds far beyond individual life, for the historical progress of the human mind consists of the forward steps that have been made in shaking off the tyranny of descriptive theories when the insight is gained that what seemed to be reality itself was only one more limited—and now obsolete—way of representing it. The advance of science consists of such liberating acts, each of which surpasses and exposes a set of previous absolutes. It is a curious comment upon our historic form of life and upon the limits it imposes upon our minds that we can thus never hope to penetrate the quasi-representational character of our current point of view until its spell is broken by cultural change.

If a mode of description must be retained because it is laid down in tradition or in sacred books, there are other means of achieving intellectual advance beyond the scriptures in which the past had believed all reality to be enshrined. Instead of committing the sacrilege of altering the canonic text we can maintain that it is meant to convey a higher allegorical or philosophical truth, so that its position is confirmed but its claim abridged by establishing its representational state. Through this pious subterfuge, religion provides the gap between the likeness and its referent without which representation cannot exist, and thus escapes from the need to regard the text as identical with reality itself. Without abolishing the authority upon which it rests, it is able to meet new intellectual demands.

Assume now that the distinction between a likeness and its referent has collapsed because the interpretant fails to understand that the picture which he beholds is only one of a group of iconographically kindred works of art. There are then two ways in which he may conceive of the identity of the likeness with the entity represented: either as a fusion with its subject, a miraculous event which may bridge great distances in space and in time, or as the much easier fusion of the work of art with its import, i.e. with an entity that has its being within the likeness itself. Of these the first reaction is a primitive one that overreaches itself in its crude assumption of magic relationships, whereas the second heralds a greater maturity by the very limitations which it is disposed to accept.

We have spoken above of the theory of magic identity. It postulates that in some unexplained manner the subject takes up residence in the likeness devoted to it. The result, in the case of visual images, is that they come to life as if they were the entities portrayed, and even act, responding in miraculous ways to the prayers addressed to them. Each image attains a personality of its own that distinguishes it from other idols of its kind, belying the dependence of all upon a common mythological prototype. Thus idols become local divinities and acquire rights by virtue of the peculiar link which connects superstition with parochial attitudes. The subject, on the other hand, loses the context of ideas and events in which it had lived before it was forced into an all-too-close alliance with a material embodiment. With its aloofness gone and its mental character upset, it presents itself as existing in the real world; its relation to its hypostasis can now be only one of obsession, of an in-dwelling in the actual wood or stone. No wonder that, while this conception lasts, the likeness does not need to come close to what it portrays, since its magic potency is a sufficient *raison d'être*. What we called the common basis of representation is thus seriously abridged.

But idols are inert and thus resist any effort to breathe an extraneous life into them. In order to see the identification at work with an overwhelming effect, born out of true kinship between representamen and principal, we must turn to the stage. The primary phenomenon there, with which the history of the theater begins, is the identity assumed by actor and audience alike between him and the divinity he portrays, who is believed to speak through him as through a person possessed. Nor is this identification limited to archaic times, for the sense of living a part to the point of forgetting that there is an ego, an audience, and a stage, can come to any actor at any time, although good ones know that they are trespassing upon the limits of their art as soon as they abandon conscious control. The use of the mask, widely diffused over the civilizations of the world, serves as a means of evoking the presence of powers from beyond—gods, demons, and heroes of the past— who thus enter into the performer, and the effect is reinforced because the mask itself, by the very fact that it hides and simulates, impresses man with a sense of weirdness and of strangeness. The masked person is experienced as identical with the entity he portrays, and his appearance in the course of a religious festival is apt to strike holy terror in the hearts of the other celebrants.

The reciting of mythology, finally, which is often combined with theatrical activities, usually demands that the manner of its performance must be fixed down to the minutest detail, since only thus can assurance be gained that reality itself has been caught in the recital. Its content is felt to be closer to the heart of things— whose precarious order must not be disturbed—than is the experience of everyday life, and must therefore always be conveyed by the same means. Besides these serious myths most civilizations have evolved another kind, designed to gratify imagination for its own sake, without deference to ritual ends. We know them as legends and fairy tales.

It is impossible to tell when, in the course of human events, the aesthetic attitude toward representational art emancipated itself from its mythical counterpart, since both seem always to have existed side-by-side as two different modes of identifying a likeness with its principal. That they are fundamentally different is beyond a doubt, for although primitive thought identifies a work of art with objects distant in space and in time, appreciation is content to assume a coincidence between the work of art and what it is to convey, all magical flights into the world of things being thus rigorously excluded. Even though there may be a lingering trace of interest in the subject portrayed, the work of art is now so dominant a presence that it no longer depends on linkage with things outside itself, and immanent relationships come to the fore.

Under such conditions the old identities must be recast, for it is no longer enough to insist upon the definition of the object portrayed or even upon a precise pattern of ritual observances. This crude procedure could suffice only as long as the referent was assumed to exist in the outer world, so that the likeness could merge with its subject as soon as their identical classification had been assured. Now, however, with representation imbedded in the work of art itself, there is a far-reaching logical change, which incorporates all component parts, including the elements of color and design, under the guidance of representational intent. From now on it is not the mere fact that representation has occurred which causes the fusion with the new principal, but rather the manner in which representation has been carried out. This means, in turn, that representation itself, instead of referring variously to an invariant principal, becomes the exponent of the visual and auditory means by which it is sustained.

The emphasis in the new dispensation lies upon the formal resources employed or upon what we are accustomed to call the "artistic" qualities of the work of art, i.e., those characteristics in which its uniqueness resides. We agree with a recent writer on art that these

qualities, which dwell in combinations of sounds or
forms, transmit the semblance of emotional states not
otherwise accessible to us, rendering them concrete and
articulate; and that the manner in which these are expressed provides the work of art with an innate significance that cannot be separated from it, since its presence is felt rather than demonstrable by discursive means
—a case, as the reader will observe, of intent merging
with the vehicle employed, because the latter is the only
means through which this particular content can be
conveyed.

In likenesses this "significant form" must come to
terms, in one of two ways, with whatever is represented;
representation may acknowledge the prior claims of
"significant form," or colors and lineaments may be subservient to the creation of a representational shape.
What we called the import of a work of art, the sense
that a specific representation is at hand, may precede
the analysis of constituent parts, as it often does in
the visual arts, or it may gradually emerge from the
action portrayed, as in literary works of art. What
matters is that the import will merge with the aesthetic
means, producing a situation equivalent to that which
in more primitive times overcame the tension between
likenesses and their real prototypes; only now the acknowledged uniqueness of the work of art is not the mere
result of a parochial frame of mind discounting all
rival claims by kindred works but of the specific configuration within the painting or sculpture itself. Thus
after recognition has been effected, our eye passes once
more over the areas which had helped us before to establish a preliminary identity, discovering unsuspected
details, descriptive niceties, and emphatic uses of color
and shape that had been overlooked during the first

survey, and these qualities are now combined to give to the representation an emotional tenor experienced as inherent in the work of art. It is right and normal that these expressive features should be attributed to the entity portrayed, turning it both into a vehicle and a beneficiary of significant form.

The manner of the relation between import and expression varies greatly, depending upon whether the artist is more concerned with bringing out the implications of his topic or with imposing upon it his own sovereign insight into formal relationships. He may be content with bending every compositional part toward a central aim, disposing figures and scenery so that their outlines will help to emphasize the meaning of the scene: this is the case of Giotto. Or he may be aware of a tension between import and compositional demands, playing them off against each other and thus creating a visual counterpoint between the various components of the design. This attitude, which tends to pry representation and composition apart, is found in the works of Poussin. Whichever position the artist may take, he will be concerned with casting a subject in appropriate formal terms, so that justice will be done both to its own expressive claims and to the need of balancing his means. It is always a sign of weakness or of a crisis in personal or cultural life when the artist permits a conflict to arise between preconceived shapes and the import they should have helped to convey. We then speak of a mannerist trend.

XI *Subjects and Motifs*

The last two chapters have taught us that the referent of representational art is far from being a simple thing, that it is ever ready to shift its ground and to enter into new guises and ambiguities. We must now add that we have not yet gathered up all the logical particles which go into the making of a representational work of art, and that others can be discerned on closer inspection. Obviously, before we proceed, it will be necessary to hew a path through this jungle of invisible entities.

It is tempting to begin with the artist's subject, since of all functions which we must enumerate it stands out as the most distinct—the only one whose life began before the birth of the work of art. Alas, it is also the most demanding and difficult, fraught as it is, besides its conceptual tasks, with metaphysical implications. We shall find it expedient to avoid a full discussion of it until other matters are out of the way, and to bring it in only when doing so will help to elucidate kindred interests. Nor can we hope to do much better with what may be called "the artist's subject seen through the eye of the interpretant," since this projection of a latter-day point of view upon the past is too indirect to command our interest at this stage.

There remains then "the subject as proffered by the work of art," or, as we shall say, its denoted subject. It is this subject to which we allude when, without attempting to peer into the artist's mind, we speak of a picture as representing a view of Haarlem, Achilles battling Hector before the walls of Troy, or the Madonna and Child. In each case the subject is not contained by the work of art but pointed out by it as something that has an existence apart. No matter what aspect the artist selects, what phase he portrays, and what mood he invokes, the subject will always remain, an absolute that refuses to bend before the varieties of contingent approach. And the same will be the case even when the subject stipulates a particular view such as "The Grand Canal from the Rialto bridge," for then, too, the subject still will be invariant, while the conditions of observation are apt to change. The subject thus concerns itself with things that are self-contained, complete, and independent of any point of view. Because it is set apart from the manner in which it appears to us, it matters little whether the subject is taken from the outer world, as is the case in landscape and portraiture, or whether it exists only as an idea in a human mind. In either case its aloofness persists, for subjects show themselves impervious to the manipulations that may be applied to them. Whether we choose to name or to comment, to discuss, describe, judge, or evaluate, the subjects to which these operations refer are unaffected by what is done to them, since their existence is prior to such mental activities. It is thus only an application of a more general law when we say that, as the *raison d'être* of a work of art, a subject has a being apart from any realization devoted to it. The only thing that affects this splendid isolation is the fact that a subject must be defined: an activity in the course of which the character of the subject may be sensibly changed, for every subject lives within mental co-ordinates that place it among neighboring ideas and events.

It follows from all that has been said that subjects are strongly individualized. They will accept the lesser status of members of a class only if there is no other way of defining them. The limits lie in such subjects of art as "the anatomy of the human arm" or "the flower of the Columbine," which remain legitimate only because the species which they illustrate can be regarded as fully determinate. This close definition of subjects implies that they will hold their own among kindred entities. If they were only samples of a class determined by the artist's personal proclivities, they would lose their sheltering frame of reference and become absorbed into the narrower framework of subjective experience.

What is true of the spectator's approach when he confronts the subject of a work of art, is equally true of the artist when he first comes to grips with the subject. He will experience it as an objectively-given entity so imperious and so impervious to any effort to manipulate it that it will leave him no choice but to submit to its superior requirements. Thus subjects, in the sense defined, owe little to the artist's preference, which, if allowed to interfere, would divest them of their absolute claim and degrade them, in spite of their individual shapes, into mere toys, occasions for the play of creative energies. No motif, which he himself selects because of its subjective interest, can be called a subject as here defined.

Subjects, according to this manner of thought, are topographical views as distinguished from those which have no particular locale; representations of definite historic events as against battle scenes chosen for their passion and violence; portraits meant to honor an outstanding individual as against mere studies of an appealingly expressive or exotic face. The distinction is clear and manifest, although in any given case there may be insufficient data to permit final judgment—no portrait, for instance, carries the evidence in itself that will reveal whether it was commissioned as the likeness of a particular person or whether it was undertaken on the artist's own initiative because of the appeal of the model as a type. Both approaches may intermingle in an artist's work, as they do in Rembrandt, whose interest in the hidden profundities of the human face often drove him to seek out sitters for his canvases.

A curious and radical consequence follows from the prohibition which we had to establish for the sake of iconographic purity. For once we exclude the artist's point of view, with its emphasis upon values dear to him, then we have said, in effect, that a subject, if it is to remain objective and definite, must not be permitted an artistic frame of reference. It would then seem normal and right that the privilege of choice should be given to the client, in the hope that he will be motivated by other than aesthetic interests, instead of entrusting it to the artist. Subjects, if our analysis is right, may be religious, mythological, commemorative, documentary, scientific, instructive, or anything else; only they must not be artistic if they are to preserve their logical identity. It will then be the painter's or sculptor's task, and the test of his ability, to subordinate himself to the subject and to cast its values (which by definition are external to art) in sensory form. The only exception occurs when the client, in choosing the subject, is himself dominated by artistic perceptions, a case so rare and so much at odds with his usual social role that it has remained without influence.

At any rate, the primacy of the nonaesthetic subject is borne out by historic evidence, for the vast majority of the works of art, in all civilizations, have been at the service of nonaesthetic concerns, usually of religious interests. Art has fared well under this foreign yoke, for its power has grown and its range increased as it has stretched its means to meet heteronomous demands. It has shown itself capable of grappling with values as extreme as the sublime or the mystically remote; and while such ennobling influences prevailed, the artist's ambitions were lifted to their peak, producing not only the most comprehensive works of art but also the most profound and vigorous. Compared to what has thus been achieved under outside stimulus, any retreat to a mere autonomy of art is likely to be an impoverishment, since it limits what can be attained to the narrower field of the artist's sensibilities.

To say what the context of primary subjects may be would mean to enumerate all the modes of discourse in which the mind can engage. It may be determined by a spatial reference, as is a view of Haarlem, with its environment of canals and plains; or by a historical one, as is a representation of the battle of Actium; or again it may be philosophic, scientific, or magic. Various interpretations of a given work of art will proceed from different assumptions as to its context. Thus Velazquez's famous picture "The Spinners," which to a seventeenth-century beholder represented the contest of Minerva and Arachne, came to be viewed as nothing more than the interior of a tapestry workshop two hundred years later, when Ovidian fables were no longer generally known; and the Middle Ages regarded the equestrian monument of Marcus Aurelius in Rome as a portrait of Constantine the Great, because to the pious pilgrim's mind the Christian frame of reference seemed the most appropriate one. It is the particular task of the iconographer to uncover such errors by steeping himself in the mental climate of the past so as to restore the original context within which these works were created. Only after he has accomplished this will he be able to arrive at a correct interpretation of the subject.

Plainly, if the subject is that which a picture denotes, there must be connotations to expand and support its all too narrow reference. Likenesses, unlike concepts, whose field of expansion is mental, characteristically present their connotations in sensory form, it being their purpose to make manifest whatever the subject involves. This is what had been the artist's aim from the moment when he set out to create a work of art; the beholder's experience should confirm that the object before him gives substance to whatever the subject implies. Thus the subject will merge with the completed work of art, unless it presents itself in a shape so devious and erratic as to be at odds with the connotations that exist in the spectator's mind; in which case there will be a conflict between what the beholder anticipates and his actual experience of the work of art.

Connotations, in turn, have a way of passing over

into the field of reference, so that one cannot always distinguish between the expansion of a given term and its legitimate environment. Do the connotations of the battle of Actium include the reasons why it was fought, the preparations for the clash, its immediate aftermath, and the expanse of sea in which the conflict took place? Can one think of Haarlem in the great period of Dutch art and omit the life sheltered within its walls, its customs and laws, and its relation to the surrounding fertile plains? Obviously, there is no clear-cut line of demarcation, and the boundary between connotations and their frame of reference will have to remain indeterminate. The environment, too, consists of terms with their own outer field of logical expansion; so that, unless the process is stopped, the definition of a subject tends to swell until it comprises the entire world.

For the artist this openness is a source of opportunity, enabling him to reject or include and thus to mould the implications of his task, until a definite interpretation is formed. There will always be some artists—they are particularly frequent in archaic times—who try to represent only a minimum of what is being implied, limiting themselves to a bare statement without visible reference to a historical or spatial setting, as in Early Greek and in some types of Byzantine and Romanesque art. Such austerity eliminates every trace of an environment, and thus confines the action it portrays to a dimensionless realm beyond space and time. But neither the Greek nor the Medieval world cared to retain this extreme restraint, once they knew how to let the likeness expand into its context, following a tendency universal in representational art. What had been the inactive background of the event now became the sector of the world against which its movement was outlined, a hinterland whose elaboration threatened at times to engulf the action portrayed. During the Northern Renaissance, a stage was reached when it became difficult to tell whether the subject of a picture was a landscape enriched by an incidental image of St. George, or whether it still was the ancient hagiographic theme. This predicament could only be resolved by choosing the landscape itself as a theme, exchanging the obsolete outer connotations of the past for others internal and commensurate with the present.

Where the context is intellectual and allegorical, there is a stronger tendency to be explicit, since ideas, in order to be fully understood, require the deployment of other thoughts. Here as elsewhere in representational art, a likeness may be linked with others of its kind to form a group, which will define the place of each by weaving it into a wreath of kindred works of art. Historic subjects will grow into series of consecutive events, allegories into intellectual cycles, and these in turn will tend to expand or proliferate until they fill the whole of their respective worlds. Likenesses tend, in other words, toward symbolic all-inclusiveness. Universalist by the very logic of the subjects portrayed, they only live an individual life when such logic gives way to an intuitive approach.

But context need not be confined to the mind nor even to kindred works of art, for it may equally be found in the situation surrounding the likeness. For the immigrant arriving in New York the Statue of Liberty is set in the midst of the transition which he is undergoing from the memories of an unsatisfactory past to the prospect of freedom and happiness in a new world. Her context is inseparable from the strategic place she occupies on the approaches to the American continent. Context does not mean the same, in this case, as in a landscape, a portrait, or a battle scene, whose temporal and spatial environment are on a par with the subject portrayed, for it tends to converge and accumulate and to burden the statue with its significance. It is notorious how much the presence of the statue helps to focus emotional attitudes that otherwise would run riot or be diffused: a growth of subjective response takes place at the expense of intellectual range. Thus the objective context of the statue may be said to shrink as it feeds the elements of which it is composed into an expanding psychological state.

The lesson of our example can be generalized into the doctrine that objective context contracts when there is an increase in subjective appeal. In the field of religious art, likenesses, in order to enter the devotional life, will forego their traditional historic setting: the Lamentation of Christ becomes the *Pietà*, stark, lonely, and a call to compassion, and the Lord's Supper may be condensed to an abbreviated image of Christ and St. John in which history is canceled out for the sake of a stronger appeal to the worshipper's devotion. A narrowing of visual and historic range is thus used to intensify emotional attitudes.

The denoted subject, so we may summarize, is something well localized and circumscribed, occupying a definite place within its own set of co-ordinates. Since it is accustomed to raise absolute claims, it does not readily come to terms with those limited perspectives and points of view that make up the artist's domain.

There is a fundamental change as soon as the artist shifts from objective and categorical demands to the freedom of suiting his own interests. The nature of motifs is most easily understood as we follow the painter in his search, observing how he stops to sketch here an intimate corner in the woods, there the hurry and bustle of a market place, or again the heavy curves of a piece of drapery; each of these is a configuration of elements that corresponds to his own particular set of interests. He will choose his materials as he sees fit, and even rearrange them so that they will approximate a desired shape. He is freest in this respect when he sets up a still life, whose elements—fruit, game, or musical instruments—though inert, obey every touch of the disposing hand.

All motifs are visual particulars taken from chosen vantage points. What distinguishes them from primary subjects is that for them this one-sided approach is a method and a profession of faith rather than a concession to human finiteness. Whereas primary subjects exist relative to themselves and to their mental and physical environment, motifs have no other affinities than with the artist's eye and his eagerness for visual experience. Thus when he goes out to hunt for them, his quarry are not things as they are in themselves but odd views and appealing aspects, which catch his eye because of the creative possibilities he finds in them. He will obtain the sensations he seeks by taking objects from a favorable side or posing and combining them effectively. Not by chance was the rise of motifs accompanied by a marked increase in the painter's awareness of his visual environment.

Motifs are thus the prime matter of the artist's craft, the inspiration on which he will draw even when confronted with a task that transcends them. No subject can be realized without the aid of this treasure of sensory data laid down in sketches and memories. The whole range of religious and mythological art subsists upon the record obtained while observing man's immediate environment. Motifs will even insinuate themselves into portraiture, for while the subject is guaranteed by the sitter's identity, the artist is often free to select the pose he prefers. Nor does the medieval copyist form an exception; he, too, ultimately depends on nature, although his work is removed from direct observation by several relays. The copyist himself, we must admit, was probably unaware of this dependence, for to him motifs were simply part of the subject he was copying.

But motifs gradually emancipated themselves as the artist's autonomy increased; they emerged at first in the form of landscape, still life, and genre scenes, from the corners where they had been tucked away under the supremacy of iconographic art. A significant change took place when they began to supersede subjects as defined in the older sense, and to establish themselves in their position of privilege. At that moment the pinpointing of experience comes to an end, for motifs—secondary topics, as they may be called—tend to be accidental and indifferent members, despite their intrinsic interest, of a class corresponding to the artist's subjective propensities. They are, to fall back upon our previous terms, correlatives of drives; and drives, as we know, have little to do with individuals, since their only aim is the attainment and use of desirable particulars. Thus motifs are bound to lose that logical distinctiveness which all primary topics can claim, since they tend to be anonymous entities that might have remained entirely obscure had not the artist cared to bring them to light. Among them are such humble things as kitchen utensils, the view of a room, or a stretch of park land under the summer sun. None of these can boast a definite place in an ordered intellectual universe, and their chief appeal is thus to sensory memories. To try to establish their identities, as was done with some of the motifs used by Cezanne and the Impressionists, is idle and useless.

Thus motifs become topics in their own right, while the artist's new task consists of treating them with the same attention and deference accorded to primary subjects. Seen from the vantage point of the finished work of art, the transition, which we described as a sudden breach, is so gradual that it has long gone unobserved. The ontological situation also persists, for the spectator, accustomed to seeing aspects as the outer surface of things, will refuse to give the rank of a subject to mere appearances. The topic will thus automatically reside in the body or group of bodies which the surface reveals. Only a very one-sided stress upon sensation for its own sake, as embodied in a title of an appropriate kind, will make us forsake a well-set perceptual routine and let the conditions of observation partake in the definition of the subject portrayed. When this occurs we are close to the concept of the picturesque, which regards the world as composed of particular views, each so one-sided, unreal, and subjectively placed, that it might in turn have been derived from a picture picturesquely conceived.

Two developments result from the new appeal of sensory memories. One of these is the decline of all cyclical tendencies, impossible where there are no bearings within clear-cut mental co-ordinates. The work of art will now be a lonely and isolated thing, incapable of co-operating with others toward a common significance—predestined, if you will, to decorate rooms or to hang in unrelated series upon museum walls.

The other development is more vital and positive,

since the range of its influence affects the aesthetic attitude. We saw that as long as primary subjects prevailed, this attitude had been blended with nonaesthetic
interests; that pictures served devotional, pedagogic,
and commemorative purposes, such being the nature of
their mental environment. Now, however, under the rule
of the contingent and fortuitous, this subservience has
come to an end, since no logical charge can be placed
upon a likeness without precise identity. A still life, to
cite the most obvious case, is merely a random collection
of random elements, and thus cannot claim that focused
significance which could locate it within a conceptual
frame of reference. But because it is a mere sensuous
offering and as such without a clear-cut logical place,
a still life possesses a peculiar attractiveness. It is the
ideal correlative of any attitude that disregards all
background requirements and strides immediately toward an aesthetic experience. It may thus appeal to
purist tendencies as a shining example of art without
conceptual entanglements, or to use the well-coined
nineteenth-century phrase: art for art's sake.

Thus we arrive at the most recent consequence of
the rise of motifs, which is the abandoning of almost all
contexts, even subjective ones, in modern abstract art.
Clearly, if the motif subsists in the artist's own domain,
subject to his every whim, then he is free not only to
make his choice, but also to treat it as he pleases—
an attitude which may receive encouragement precisely
from his experience with still life, which flatters the
affirmation of the will be permitting the shuffling of its
constituent parts. Thus in the new artistic world there
is no court of appeal against arbitrariness, so that the
artist may proceed to destroy and then to rearrange
according to his formal insights what once had been

the world of recognizable form. Before, under the firm and beneficent rule of iconography, no such radicalism had been able to arise, since subjects had been logically paramount and thus could insist upon obedience and adequacy. They had been so secure against violence that they had at times approached the threshold of the abstract—witness the example of Irish Early Medieval art—without fear of being pushed across.

We must add that context and identity can be almost lost even when the work of art retains some semblance of representational shape. We speak then of decorative pattern and ornament. When the shape of animals and plants appears in the vocabulary of these arts, the concern is not with what they are in themselves, since they serve as material for a play of lines that may twist them, ravel them into knots, and so disintegrate their familiar forms that they can hardly be recognized. Any of those contexts in which they had been previously known may thus be effectively destroyed. They can be made to repeat themselves, either symmetrically or *seriatim* in rhythmic rows, in plain disregard of whatever place they may hold in any kind of natural universe. There is then a complete equivalence between such pseudo-representational shapes and systems of abstract lines, as long as each serves the same functional interests. It is worthwhile to observe that even now, when meaning is at its lowest ebb, there is a context of a sort, it being impossible for the human mind to be cognizant of anything without relating it to some kind of environment. However, with all other connections cut, the new context is now of a purely formal kind, relating pattern or ornament to the object which these shapes decorate. Ornament is thus a means of emphasis, a tool in the creation of a formal hierarchy. It will serve its function best when it remains subservient, with little stress upon assertive representational qualities.

We have assumed until now that all likenesses, unless they are ornaments pure and simple, possess a subject that can be ascertained no matter whether it belongs to the order of iconography or to that of motifs in the sense in which that term has been defined. This assumption must be modified now, for while it holds of most works of the visual arts, it does not apply to a large part of literature. What is the subject of Hamlet? Does it lie in the chronicle from which the story was drawn? One would then have to believe that there is a radical difference between a play based upon an existing anecdote and another that has been freely invented. Is the subject given by the title of the play? No, for the name says nothing about the plot within which the subject is lodged. Shall we then seek the topic in a condensed version of the text? Not unless we are ready to open the doors to a critical free-for-all, since we realize that nobody can know how far he should condense and what he should stress or omit. Such abbreviation would be advisable only if we could be certain of the true content of Shakespeare's play, but about this point there has been a long and notoriously inconclusive debate.

There is thus no doubt that a literary work of art is usually without a subject that can be ascertained, much as our feeling may suggest what it was that the artist has tried to convey. Subject and content tend to merge, since both have grown in concentric rings around the same unnamed core.

The process of creation in literature confirms this analysis, for its subject is apt to remain in flux or even to change identity unless the author undertakes in advance to adhere strictly to a preconceived scheme. Thus vast stretches of a literary work may be woven out of suggestions contained in previous events, and the course of its action may be sensibly changed because the individualities of the fictional characters and their interplay demand a modification in its development. Representation will thus assert itself at the expense of the over-all subject, not, however, without exchanging a general dependence for a relation to minor subordinate topics, some of which will have arisen within the territory of the abandoned over-all scheme. Any awareness of subject will cease if the artist's work is created in the heat of a single rapid flash of insight, as is sometimes the case in lyrical poetry.

We thus arrive at the parting of the ways between literary and visual art: the former is able to produce without previous specification, to invent and to evolve new things in accordance with the promptings of the imagination, whereas the latter is much more restrained, since it must cater to types, to pre-existing divisions which alone are the starting points of the artist's work; the former is plastic and open to change, the latter frozen into logical areas.

It is thus not surprising to see that the real initiative in the development of representation is reserved for literature, which alone is sufficiently free and elastic to create novelty; and that the visual arts were for long its humble dependents, limited to the supplementary task of making palpable what language had been the first to formulate. It is not a matter of chance that Homer and the Bible antedate by many centuries the development of the visual arts that were founded upon them and which drew countless subjects from these store-

houses of ideas and episodes. Nor should we be astonished to observe that the visual arts remained indebted
to literary models until they began to emancipate themselves by learning to rely on motifs as well as on iconographic types. The rarest thing in the world of art is
a man who can produce both poetry and painting, relating them in one incandescent unity of experience, as
did William Blake.

That painting and sculpture could represent anything at all without recourse to either a motif or a
subject would have been denied until recently, accustomed as we are to accept the implicit distinction between art and literature. The change came only with
the advent of modern art; for if anything unites most
of its various trends, it is the fact that, whether abstract or not, they propose to accomplish their aims
without submitting to what is now frowned upon as the
former tyranny of subject matter. But the emancipation has been gained at a price: if it is true that there
is a link between intelligibility and the primacy of topics
—and I implied that in my theory of contexts—then
we must conclude that it is impossible to evade their
control without a corresponding loss of meaning. Thus
surrealist pictures represent we know not what, within
we do not know what universe of discourse, even their
creator being unable to explain what he wanted to convey. While well rid of what partisans describe as foreign
and extraneous, such works have been set free by sacri-
ficing coherence.

It is not difficult to understand why there should
be an affinity between the visual arts and the predominance of subjects while there is no corresponding affinity in the field of literature. In language, terms are
so defined that they will retain their individual identity

even though combined with other terms. Within a sentence or paragraph each word will remain relatively independent and articulate, while contributing its appointed share toward the building of a common significance. As a result, language is able to undertake the creation of novelty by subsuming new groupings of words under a new logical synthesis. The visual arts, on the other hand, do not possess this flexibility, and their offerings must be accepted *en bloc*. If a given interpretation is to take effect, it must pertain to entire entities and groups, whose subdivisions are to be understood in terms of their common topic. Thus literature can be spontaneous as long as it obeys syntactic rules, because it arises directly out of the very matrix of thought; while it is normal in the visual arts that creation should evolve from a pre-existing nucleus. Consider in addition to this that ideas, in order to avoid being absorbed into the stream of psychic events, must detach themselves as members of a world of intersubjective thought. It follows that subjects can function as such only if they are social currency, well-wrapped packages of thought, which anybody may utilize by simply acquainting himself with their context; whereas germinal ideas in literature, being blurred and indistinct, remain the author's exclusive property.

Thus, because of their social task, the topics of the visual arts are especially sensitive to the interests that motivate a group, for they are coinage only as long as the framework of thought that holds them together remains inviolate. Primary subjects presuppose a public so prepared and perhaps even indoctrinated from early youth that it will feel entirely at home in their particular world, able to recognize them without recourse to lengthy explanations and scholarly research;

and they will begin to wither away when they lose that leaven of interest which had kept them alive in the public mind. Few will withstand the slow wear and tear of routine, and all of them are bound to disappear once a tradition has run its course, leaving only a small and powerless coterie that remembers their original significance. To impose new subjects on a public that is not prepared, as the Romantic painters did in trying to gain acceptance for anecdotes from the national past, is possible only if lengthy explanations are provided in print.

It is necessary to add that when primary subjects dwindle because an established system of interests has come to nought, motifs are usually ready to fill the gap, since they demand no more from the interpretant than a memory of common visual elements. They are the lowest denominators of representational art, the dead level to which it may always fall once one of the great traditions has collapsed. Even though the comprehension of iconography may be lost, a representation of ordinary things will always retain its interest. Thus when the tradition of the academies, in whose shade primary subjects made their last stand, had given out, motifs of daily life took possession of the field of art—denoting the loss of a generally acceptable framework to which art could have clung instead of retreating to the refuge of the familiar and obvious.

Our argument has now reached a point where we must acquaint ourselves with one more logical component of representational art. This, to distinguish it from what a picture denotes, we shall call its designated subject, i.e., its internal reference to an established iconographic type. That such a reference exists was im-

plied as soon as we came to realize that creation in the
visual arts is usually compelled to range around pre-
existing themes; every one of these topics generates a
corresponding class of works of art, to which the individual picture will have to adhere. Thus a painting will
not only represent the Madonna, referred to in the
Gospels and the Apocrypha and venerated by members
of the Orthodox and Catholic church, but it will also
belong to an iconographic type called "the Madonna,"
which we put in quotes to indicate that we are now concerned with a conventional type rather than with realities. In a similar sense we are accustomed to say that
a picture "is"—notice the revealing manner of speech—
"a martyrdom of St. Catherine" or, in the case of
motifs, "a landscape," "a still life," or "a view of the
Mont St.-Victoire." In each case the reference is caught
within the compass of art, and no attempt is made to
penetrate to realities beyond. Even when we say that
a picture *represents* "the Madonna," keeping the quotes
while changing the verb, we have merely asserted in an
ambiguous way that it belongs to a class of representational entities. Otherwise we would have to assume that
the quotes indicated an individual name such as "the
Moses of Michelangelo"; or that they betokened that
neutrality of mind which refuses to take a stand because the subject may be alien to our civilized ways.
Witness the manner in which we say, without committing
ourselves, that a painting represents "the Buddha Ava-
lokiteshvara" or "the mechanics of heaven according to
Ptolemy."

The designated subject is thus a conventional type,
devoid of that reality which denoted subjects can claim.
It is complete, as far as its nature allows, as soon as
it has made itself known through the recognition of

characteristic lineaments; and it must rely, in consequence, for whatever transcends this limited role, upon
the denoted subject with which it is aligned. No artistic
type would be more than an empty exercise in iconographic distinctions and subtleties if it did not draw
its life—its authorization, if you will—from a higher
quarter; for all potential value resides in and spreads
from the denoted subject. Thus the artistic type of the
Madonna owes all that it can express of purity and
maternal love to the subject as evolved by the doctrine
of the Church and by generations of Christian worship-
pers; and the same applies to the various subordinate
types, in which some of her qualities are condensed into
imagery such as "the Madonna on the Moon" or "the
Virgin of Humility." All of these, however distinct as
conventional types, are only variants of one comprehensive theme from which they derive their radiance
and vitality.

We must conclude that, although closely aligned,
subjects and types may have different amplitude, and
that types may be confined to the role of presenting
in concentrated form aspects and sectors of a vaster
theme. Although it is true that these types become subjects of their own, their context consists mainly of
elements drawn from the sphere of the denoted subject.
The context of "the Madonna of Humility" is essentially the same as that which informs far simpler iconographic types, only that here the attributes surrounding the Virgin lend accent and explicitness to some of
her traditional traits.

Other relations between subject and type are less
one-sided than this, because they deal not with values,
which always proceed from a given source, but with
refinements of logical emphasis. If we ask which is prior

in the experience of the interpretant, the type to which a painting belongs or the subject which it denotes, the answer will depend on whether the subject has been found in the outer world—e.g., a landscape or a contemporary face—or whether it is of a traditional kind. In works of art whose arrangement reflects established usage—this is true of most works dealing with religious and historic themes—the designated subject is paramount, for the signs by which we recognize them—i.e., the connotations of the designated theme—must first be applied to the type before we can inform ourselves about the reality beyond. It is because a statue represents "St. Peter," a traditional type distinguished by his keys and curly beard, that it also represents the apostle Peter, historically known as the tempestuous and faithful follower of the Lord; and the same applies wherever recognition depends upon the presence of significant traits stabilized by tradition.

It follows that whenever we have a topic of this kind, the commonly-understood marks of recognition connect the work of art first of all with its type and only secondarily with its denoted subject. A little thought will yield the further result that the rationale follows the same preordained path and rises through the type to the denoted subject beyond. When we say, in accordance with our own theory, that a statue of St. Peter is one of many of the same kind which potentially or actually exist, we obviously mean that it belongs to an iconographic type whose members all display the same conventional signs. The only amendment that needs to be made states that the same subject may be rendered by several types, if such an anomaly is demanded by historical circumstances. A case in point is the medieval pictures of Classical divinities, which took on entirely different shapes depending upon whether the tradition to which the artist conformed was the literary one of learned mythography or a visual one derived from actual images.

If the likeness is no more than a factual report about the appearance of things in the outer world, then both the rationale and the common basis constituted by the marks of recognition refer to the denoted subject. Thus a portrait does not resemble some shadowy secondary type, fit only to interfere between it and its principal, but its sitter, who is also the common source of all other likenesses that may be made of him. And the same can be said of pictures of a generic but factual type, such as those which we conveniently call "a still life" or "a landscape" and which we are accustomed to treat as if their immediate subject were known, applying both the common basis and the rationale directly to the image at hand. A type, then, wherever the factual orientation prevails, is merely a collection of representational works of art united by a common allegiance to one denoted subject. It is only in this limited sense that we are justified in saying that all the existing portraits of Lincoln, whether paintings, etchings, or photographs, constitute a circumscribed pictorial type. Obviously where such conditions prevail the designated subject is bound to be weak. It tends to be absorbed into the denoted subject and to remain unobserved.

Before we abandon the relation between denoted and designated themes, it is necessary to cast a glance at the bearing this relation has upon the distinction between signs and representational images. Readers familiar with semantic theory will have noticed that the two afore-mentioned terms are the same that are employed in explaining the functions of conventional signs.

This is not by chance, for we shall endeavour to show that their conformity is close, and that conventional signs are an impoverished form of what we called iconographic types. To effect the transformation it is enough to take a group of likenesses belonging to a given type and to suppress their freedom by substituting an arbitrarily-chosen identity for the resemblance which they all share (and which connects them with their principal). We propose, in other words, to eliminate the common basis which unites the dependents of a given type and whose task it is to guarantee their natural diversity. All other elements which go into the making of a representational work of art we propose to leave undisturbed.

As an immediate result of this single but radical mental act we will have turned representation into sign function, for what remains after the operation is no different from hieroglyphic script. In the new situation, sounds, gestures, and likenesses, provided they show certain common diacritical marks, will be defined as identical, so that they will always evoke the same intellectual response. All members of this infinite group—and here we see that the rationale has survived—are still aligned by the fact that they are multiple dependents of a single entity; only their relation to that entity has ceased to be a natural one, since it is created by rule and arbitrary choice. In addition, signs, like pictures belonging to iconographic types, possess a designated principal, which determines their conventional referent —for the word subject cannot here be applied—within a language, so that the referent can be looked up in a dictionary. And finally, again in the same sense as likenesses, signs have a denoted principal which connects them by the designated term with the world of ideas and realities. Only the connotations of signs suffer from the operation performed, for they cannot be embodied as they are in representational works of art, since signs lack a natural connection with their principal and thus must be externally applied by the mind. The parallelism with representation holds nevertheless, for the formal definition of a linguistic term, containing no more than the means by which recognition is attained, corresponds to the connotations of an iconographic type, whereas the real definition is similar to the context which helps to keep a denoted subject in place.

It is thus clear that linguistic signs are no more than truncated members of iconographic types, except that, being conventional throughout, they are able to extend their rule beyond the historic and remote to all things capable of being discussed. We must conclude that what holds of individual signs is true of the category to which they belong, and that thus the entire linguistic field is subject to representational laws; or, in other words, that semantics, as long as it deals with conventional signs, is subordinate to the science of representation which we are trying to build. If this is true, then it will be necessary to revise some of the basic assumptions of contemporary thinking.

We do not pretend to know what concrete events in the history of human thought may originally have led to the transformation of representamina into signs, since the time when the change occurred antedates any recorded linguistic text. Iconographic types, as long as their visual character is retained, can, of course, only be turned into hieroglyphs. We leave it to the specialists to determine to what degree the so-called sentence words, which occur in certain archaic languages, can be regarded as representamina sufficiently compact to be audible equivalents of early forms of the visual arts.

After passing the various phases which a subject undergoes while it still remains distinct and separate, we have now reached the point—which we attained before in the context of other questions—when the subject begins to melt into the sensory evidence. Not all likenesses are capable of arriving at this stage, for notations, maps, and diagrams, which are too prosaic to be alluring to the eye, must forego this immediate aesthetic appeal. Unable to justify their task on the basis of their meager appearance, they are compelled to concentrate entirely on what they denote; and it is, in fact, a condition of their pedagogic success that the message they are trying to convey not be obscured by an undue display of surface qualities. Diagrams are not even types in the usual sense, since as long as the same numerical ratios are retained they may point toward several referents, reversing the connection which normally exists between the designated types and their representatives. A single diagram, with its elements unchanged, can express relations as diverse as those between social position and expenditure or between electrical charge and viscosity.

When representation becomes a surface phenomenon, its subject does not cease to exist (how could it, considering the retentiveness of the mind?), but its function is changed so that it will be subservient to the work of art instead of dominating it. As soon as we concentrate our attention upon the import of works of art, subjects turn into names; they abandon that implied generality which had assured their rule over groups of representamina, and attach themselves to individual entities. They have no other choice, for with the work of art logically and visually paramount the subject's only hope of survival is to accept a diminished role. Thus while beholding a given work of art we may let both the subject and the type evaporate, replacing them with the name by which the painted or sculpted figure may be identified. It bespeaks the purely external nature of names that, apart from applying to iconographic details, they may be attached to entire works of art, objects which bulk in the physical world and of which we speak, thinking of their place in museums, as the "Apollo Belvedere" or "The Jewish Bride."

Names apply only to unanalyzed wholes. They will shrink back to their former rank and requalify as subjects if we focus upon internal details to find out why a given designation has been employed. The purest and most characteristic names are those which are mere tags, good enough to insure an identity but without any bearing upon the internal qualities of the work of art. They are more frequent in literature than they are in sculpture and painting, because literary subjects are so impalpable and diffuse that they cannot be easily summarized. It is only the recent vogue for unintelligible forms that has brought pure tags to the fore in the visual arts, presenting us with such meaningless or misleading names as Dali's "The Persistence of Memory" or Picasso's "Les Demoiselles d'Avignon."

Iconographic types may undergo transformations of their own as soon as subjects become names, for then their visual form is set free to combine with other iconographic types. We speak of formulas if such shapes take on a rigid visual form which persists in spite of cultural and artistic change. Among the themes thus perpetuated by the continuity of visual types there often reigns a tenuous affinity of thought, which may form the historic link between them. Thus Christianity, when it needed an art of its own, availed itself of existing pagan formulas, turning the image of the sacred ruler into that of Christ and transforming tribute-bearing barbarian kings into the Magi before the new-born Child. An even more dogged persistence of visual formulas can be seen in symbols, which often retain their validity in the midst of religious change because their meaning is so ambiguous and complex. Thus the visual formula of the Tree of Life survived its transformation from a token of fertility into that of the inner life that is within the believer's grasp if he avails himself of the benefits proffered to him by the self-sacrifice of Christ. Other symbols such as the swastika or the wheel have been in use since prehistoric times, gathering up new meanings as they evolved, and leading to an unprecedented accumulation of thought in the rose window, i.e., the wheel design applied to the Christian church architecture. It is also true, on the other hand, that visual formulas, because of their relative independence from the meaning they convey, may lose all connections with a definite iconographic type, in which case they may still survive a long time as ornaments. Many of the formulas created by ancient Oriental art, among them the tree flanked by two symmetrically-confronted beasts and Gilgamesh strangling two lions with his arms, continued to be employed, thousands of years after their subjects had been forgotten, as decorative designs in Oriental and Western textiles.

It can also happen that a new visual shape, instead of being the residue of an iconographic type, results from a spontaneous mental act, in which case its identity must be confirmed by repeating the same likeness in various ways and endowing it with a name before it can become established as a new type. (A mere result of haphazard activity, such as a doodle, a visual *aperçu*, or an image obtained by surrealist means, is incapable of acquiring such an identity, since it is too fleeting and vaporous to yield a repeatable shape.) Some of the fantastic beasts of the past, such as dragons, griffons, and centaurs, may well have come into existence in this way instead of being first conceived in linguistic terms and then handed over to the artist to cast into visible form. If so, they were created not by consulting a subject in advance but as the result of man's ability spontaneously to produce representational shapes. Interestingly enough, they soon acquired an imputed reality that endowed them with a mythological identity.

Similar cases may be found on all levels of representational activity: the mere fact that a thing is stated, whether in linguistic or visual terms, even the fact that a mere concept of it can be formed, endows it with a degree of reality sufficient to ensure its existence for centuries. Most mythologies are made of such tenuous stuff. And it becomes the task of any post-mythological age either to debunk the material deposited in its lap, as children do with Santa Claus, or to vindicate its content by allegorical interpretation. The only way to avoid this unpleasant alternative, if we want to be neither brutal nor insincere, is to transform such materials into the free play of art.

Subject Functions:

ALLUSION, DESCRIPTION,
EXPLANATION, COMMENTARY

Before we proceed, we must ask whether we
were within our rights when we identified the subject
known to the interpretant with that which the artist had
to face. Can we always tell, without drawing upon supplementary evidence, what logical phase of a subject a
painter had in mind at the moment when he set out to
work? The answer is clearly in the negative, for the
subject—or the reality to which it refers—does not
necessarily possess the same comprehensiveness as the
version of it supplied by the work of art. It may not be
easy, therefore, to tell at what stage in the sensory evolution of a theme the artist's work had actually set in.
Thus when we have a picture of a mill near a stream,
dark with glowering skies overhead, we cannot say

whether it had been the artist's job to capture this particular mood, whether he was required to represent this particular locale, irrespective of weather and time of day, whether he merely set out to paint a mill—any mill—near a stream, or perhaps just a landscape without further ado.

Similar ambiguities are not hard to find. With only the picture for a guide we cannot tell how much of its surface is occupied by the subject itself; whether, for instance, the artist was free to surround the Madonna with flowers and trees or whether these paraphernalia form part of one overarching iconographic type. We must be equally diffident of the element of time and thus cannot say, on the sensory evidence alone, whether a given action had to be rendered at a specific and predetermined moment or whether the matter of timing was left to the artist's choice. Subjects and motifs are no better defined: without external clues we cannot decide whether the "Mars" by Velasquez is what the title suggests, i.e., a Classical God, though one who has fallen on evil days, or whether we should trust the evidence of our eyes, which show a man picked up from the streets and supplied with incongruous pagan attributes. None of these uncertainties could be removed without research into the circumstances under which the work in question was created or, failing that, into the pictorial habits prevailing during the artist's lifetime.

It will be equally difficult to find out, if indeed such factors are within our reach, how far the development of a topic had progressed when the patron entrusted it to the artist's care, for the former may have suggested only its most general outline, expecting the latter to render it concrete. The commission, as stated, may have been one for "a landscape," "a still life," or "an allegorical scene," giving the artist full discretion to implement the wide range of choice left open to him. The "mill near a stream" introduced before may thus have been commissioned by a patron who, in a fit of romantic gloom, specified that it should be a dark and foreboding scene; but it may equally well be that the patron's thought was merely of a favorite locale and that it was the artist who decided to paint the picture in a somber mood. Nor can we omit a third possibility, historically the most likely one by far, that the artist did not do the picture for any particular patron at all, since he was a free lance and himself an adherent of the Romantic school. In any event, the patron's role is not to prescribe a fully-individualized work of art—for he could neither conceive nor impose such a thing—but merely to specify certain well-defined traits. No matter how much he may attempt to furnish details, the instructions he can provide will never approach the complete fusion of parts which only the artist can achieve.

The greatest possible latitude prevails when a true universal is given as a theme, so that the artist will be free to decide whether to treat it in a purely allegorical vein or to exemplify it through individual scenes. Thus if the subject is "the fertility of the earth," some may want to handle it in traditional terms, conveying the idea by means of a personification such as a lady with cornucopia in hand; others might want to render the connotations of the theme by expanding it panorami-cally, in the manner of the American "post-office style" of the 1930's, presenting a survey of agricultural labors and of the bounty liberally supplied by the soil; or again an artist might want to contract the theme into a single pregnant scene, such as a still life with vegetables and fruit, or a view of yellow fields waiting to be harvested.

In the examples discussed, we note an ever-widening gulf between the artist's and the patron's world, until in the last case there remains only a tenuous link between what the patron proposes and what the artist supplies. Where things have come to such a logical pass, the term "given subject" does not suffice, for it has been split into two component parts: the over-all subject, which the patron handed out, and the real one, which the artist evolved. But it also needs to be said that such a dichotomy is rare, since it presupposes, on the patron's part, great uncertainty of mind and aesthetic indifference—failings which individuals hardly ever display to the same extent as do juries and official committees.

As we contemplate the vagaries of subjects, we are bound to ask what fixes them at a particular stage rather than another that is equally within logical range. The answer will lead us into a field upon which we have hardly touched, knowing that if we were to give an adequate exposé we would have to wander far from our path. The position of the subject in a representational scheme depends on the value embodied in it and on the manner in which that value is set. In order to put our observations in their proper frame, let us first state the obvious fact that there is no subject of any kind that does not have a value imbedded in it, since nobody would dream of realizing it if it were of no interest at all. It is values that light the way when subjects rise to historical eminence; and it is values again that drag them down when they themselves have to leave the stage. Values give subjects their weight, they maintain their subjects' appeal and safeguard them against obscurity.

Very naturally, then, values come to the fore when

an accent is to be placed within a pictorial scheme. Take
the "Mars" by Velazquez discussed before: the answer to
the question of what was in the painter's mind as he em-
barked upon this pathetic and derisive work depends
on where the original value was placed, whether it re-
sided in the mythological world or in that of everyday
life. A third possibility remains, again within a value
scheme: namely, that the subject in the artist's mind
was from the start a mockery of the Olympian gods, in
the manner of Lucian's sarcastic attacks, in which case
his task was to state a value and to destroy it at once.
Or to use an example from a very different sphere which
presents us, not with alternatives, but with a question
of emphasis: among the iconographic types that realize
the Last Supper in art there is one showing St. John,
the favorite disciple, as he leans his head trustingly
against the chest of the Lord, as described in the Gospel
text according to St. John. The question of what the
given subject was must again be decided on the basis of
the value implied: did the patron merely want a representation of the Last Supper, leaving the choice of
iconographic type to the artist, or was his affection for
St. John and his desire to succeed him in the love of the
Lord so great that he insisted upon the telling detail?
In the latter case the subject, properly named, would be
"The Last Supper according to St. John," whereas in
the former the figure of the apostle would be displayed
merely to implement a representation conceived in more
general terms.

We must confess at this point that what we have
argued up to now was intended merely to prepare the
way for a further case, in which the relation of the
given to the apparent subject shows itself in a new and
unsuspected light. We have taken it for granted that

the two, if they can be separated at all, refer each in its particular way to the same image, so that any conflict between them must be caused by a hitch in the transmission of thought. We shall now investigate the more difficult case of the designated subject having only an indirect bearing upon the denoted subject, so that the likeness cannot be fully understood without a transfer of ideas. In order to grasp the artist's intent, it will be necessary to be aware of the subject in both of its forms and to relate the two by interpretative thought. At the same time we shall also deal with likenesses that fail to render their subject as a whole, because the latter is either so large or so complex that it cannot be fully resolved into representational shapes. In either case, the artist's designated subject remains intact, refusing to be absorbed into what the likeness actually presents. Thus it retains its logical weight, whatever aesthetic stage may have been reached, compelling us to keep it in mind while our apparent concern centers upon other things only loosely related to it. Naturally, under conditions such as these art will not rise very high, since the obligation to consider the subject at all times prevents a full unfolding of aesthetic interest. The categories of art with which we are concerned are marginal ones such as allegorical allusions, illustrations, political cartoons, and other commentaries upon contemporary events. Since all of these are intimately allied with subject functions of other kinds, we shall first try to acquaint ourselves with their general role before we focus upon their visual aspects.

That subjects need not be realized in the sense of being absorbed into surface qualities is an experience of everyday life. When several human beings converse, there will be a topic around which the discourse re-

volves, unless the speakers are so flighty and scatter-
brained that they cannot hold on to a given theme. The
subject may be argued, discussed, and exemplified, and
various opinions may be brilliantly held, but there is
one thing that is not apt to occur as long as the com-
pany is ruled by the unwritten laws of social intercourse: no speaker will be allowed to give a reasoned
exposé, a rendering so coherent and complete that the
topic will seem to have been absorbed in it. It is rather
generally understood that to lecture at social functions
is not good manners, and that the ability to give a subject its unstinted due does not suffice to qualify a man
as a conversationalist. He will have to acquire the very
different technique of seeming to leave the subject untouched while orienting his free play of words by frequent backward glances toward it. What is true of
speech in ordinary give and take will be found to hold
generally in the relation of men to the subjects of their
thought, unless they have the artist's urge and power
to penetrate and organize them. Subjects will thus tend
to rest impermeable and inert, because no effort is made
to render them articulate.

In addition there are certain modes of speech whose
logical character demands that they be pointed toward
a topic, but without transmuting it into valid sensory
shape. This is the common feature which unites functions otherwise as distinct as allusions, descriptions, explanations, and comments; all of which have a subject
which persists while their diverse operations unfold; and
which thus, instead of dissolving into their surface in
due time, compels them to remain subordinate. In each
case the subject is so near, inevitable, and complete, that
it oppresses the function beholden to it, and the function itself is so lacking in necessary detail that it can-

not stand upon its own feet. In contrast to this, wherever true representation prevails the likeness opposes the subject with a reality of its own, complete enough to be its embodiment; and it will be the subject, in this case, that will exist only in fragmentary terms once the artist has set out upon his work. All that then remains of its former status within its own ideal world is the obligation it imposes upon the artist to assure recognition by appropriate means, while it leaves him free in almost all other respects. Similarly the spectator, when confronted with the work of art, will regard the subject, whatever it may have been in itself, as a function of the likeness he beholds. There is thus a clear parting of the ways. To put the matter in concise terms, representation transmits the subject as incarnate in the work of art, while subject functions transmit only something pertaining to it.

Otherwise the afore-mentioned functions are very clearly distinct. Of allusions, for instance, it may be said that they only touch their subject from the outside, very lightly, even hesitantly, as it were, while the subject itself, if recognized at all, looms large in the hearer's mind. As a result there is a great discrepancy of weight, which, when added to the fragmentary character of allusive speech, assures the dominance of the theme alluded to. Moreover, as a mode of utterance, allusions depend on the previous presence of the subject in the hearer's mind, and thus are confined to matter recent and notorious enough to be reliably known within a given group.

Descriptions, on the other hand, aim at the totality of the object described, and thus remain internal to it. Their particular imperfection consists in their inability to give the object in the concrete, so that they must aim to approximate it as best they can through the ma-

chinery of words. Efforts to describe a landscape or a
work of art are therefore doomed to frustration unless
the speaker knows in advance that real adequacy is
beyond his means, or, for that matter, unless he possesses the gift of so transmuting what he tries to describe that he deflects our gaze from his subject to his
manner of presenting it. Some of the descriptive poems
by Rilke are of this kind. But unless such a miracle occurs, descriptions, like allusions, will merely point toward their referent, because they are defective and incomplete, while their subject basks in its own rounded
integrality.

A description is thus a representation in reverse,
and we need not be astonished to find that the boundary
line between the two may be very thin, since they are
separated mainly by a difference of emphasis. It might
be argued that a subject, once the artist ponders over
it, becomes a description of the future work of art: a
thing as yet tentative and incomplete with only its main
features clearly outlined, yet tied with every fiber to
what is about to be created. It is much less certain that
a work of the visual arts can ever be looked upon as a
description of its subject, since, in spite of the inevitable
omission of details, it renders each aspect complete,
and thus is not fragmentary in the same sense as is the
disjunctive progression of speech. The distinction between representation and description can even be carried into the literary arts, much as the two functions
then seem to converge because of their common reliance
upon the medium of words. Both will build their subject
within the dimension of time. But whereas representation is free to evolve without stating its subject in advance, description will make clear what it refers to, and

then proceed to fill in details. It is at all times tied to its theme.

While the incompleteness of descriptions is a matter of regret, something that one would like to remedy if one could, it is an essential and necessary trait in explanations, whose task it is to reduce a welter of cumbrous and enigmatic detail to the cause-and-effect relationship that brought them forth. Thus, since they lay bare the very bones of a case, explanations are even more at the mercy of their subject than are descriptions, for the subject to be explained is the sole *raison d'être* of all that is being said. It remains the paramount issue even if explanation is carried beyond its immediate range in order to avail itself of adjoining auxiliary facts.

If our thought is correct, representation cannot become identified with explanatory techniques, since both treat their subjects in mutually irreconcilable ways. But while no fusion will occur, one often finds representation, even in its visual variant, at the service of explanatory aims. Charts and diagrams will offer simplified renderings of factors in which explanation has taken an interest, reducing a problem to its easiest terms and thus enabling us to understand at one glance what it would have taken a much longer time to comprehend if the same subject had been presented by discursive means. In each case the problem to be explained is apt to be more extended and complex than the model that representation has made of it; and thus the chart may deal with a limited referent that may be no more than a skeleton of the subject seen in explanatory terms. The representation will point to its denoted principal, which will exist in its own ideal universe; the subject to be explained, on the other hand, will be real, a present and insistent thing that may possess all the muddled complexity which is the hallmark of immediate reality. Moreover, the subject may be composed of motions, stresses, and tendencies in space, which, in order to be fully explained, would require a three-dimensional model with shifting parts, so that diagrammatic representation, if it is confined to the plane, will have to resort to arrows as indicators of direction and speed.

At any rate, if an image serves as an explanatory tool, the relations within it carry the day over the entities it is designed to relate. And since relations in turn are predicates, i.e., universals not bound to any set of particular facts, such likenesses can disregard logical precedent and adjust themselves to any suitable subject, provided that it falls within the purview of their scheme. The same genealogical tree, with its branches waiting for future occupants, may thus be fit to render the relations within an ancestral group, of coal to its chemical derivatives, or of a virtue to secondary ethical attitudes. In each case the lines that mark the relationships have logical priority over the corresponding entities. Relations in turn may be transformed into tendencies and these again into actual movements without exploding the framework prepared for them, with the sole proviso that vectors, because of their directedness, must be indicated by arrows.

Thus the most abstract visual schemes are likely to serve best as explanatory tools, because they offer nothing to deflect the mind from its contemplation of relationships. It is only fair, however, to record that before they settled in their modern groove, there was a long period when visual aids availed themselves of allegorical means. Concepts were personified and their connections made manifest by assigning to each its determined place within a spatial hierarchy. Nor did this pedagogical method shrink from personalizing the concept of force, or rather the clash between vectorial trends, as can be seen from those allegorical themes which concern themselves with the battle between virtue and vice. Applying the same principle one might render the well-known parallelogram of force by two men striving in different directions, while a third, more moderate and reasonable than they, outdistances them by proceeding on a road between. The image may, to some, seem absurd. Yet it is well known that in the concept of physical force there lurked a ghost compounded of muscular strains, which survived until it was finally slain in our own days by the theory of relativity. Only the idea of using visual devices for elucidating numerical relationships seems to have originated in the modern world. It too may tend toward the use of personified shapes, but these will designate comparative quantities instead of the qualitative values of the past.

That commentaries, at least those attached to literary works, are a kind of explanation, will seem natural to most, even though their concern is with meaning rather than with the mode of operation of mental and physical schemes. But they are not explanations of the usual sort, for these must accord with the recognized nature of the thing explained, while commentaries deal with structures so uncertainly known that they admit a variety of independent approaches. Commentaries can be clearly a very personal affair—such as series of notes jotted down for a man's own enlightenment—and thus may lay much less emphasis upon the presence of the subject in the audience's mind than is the case in explanatory and allusive speech. The commentator's philosophy may affect them in various ways; and they may even be conceived with the intention of assimilating a document from the past to the requirements of a dominant modern way of thought.

More important still are the structural divergences; an explanation usually comes to grips with its subject by direct and frontal assault, while commentaries must tackle theirs in piecemeal fashion. They attach themselves to single phrases or paragraphs, disregarding the essential unity of the text under discussion. Obviously the subject looms very large, too large to be seen as a whole. Thus if a commentary were to become a representation of its subject, the commentator would first have to step back, survey the content of the subject in its entirety, rearrange it to suit his own literary bent, and then present it in new and original form. Similarly, a news commentator is expected to confine himself to his daily stint of informed remarks, since the affairs upon which he trains his pen are so close, insistent, and incomplete that an over-all exposition is beyond his ken. If he wants to go beyond the role of the commentator, by rounding out his marginal remarks into a genuine representation of events, he will have to remove himself from his recurrent chore, let things fall into scale, and allow an over-all interpretation to emerge.

Thus the ideal form of the commentary consists of a series of separate asides, none of them broad enough to serve as an embodiment of its theme. We suspect that the readiness of commentators to distort their text by squinting at it from some marginal point of view is often due to the presence of an irreducible fact so bulky that it can be tackled only from the side.

Assume now that we abandon neutrality before a given set of events because they are so close yet so malignant, unintelligible, or perverse that we can neither accept them nor push them aside. We will then react by subjective and withering remarks that embody a judgment upon unacceptable circumstance. A mild example of this is the pungent words with which Sancho Panza, entrenched in a low form of common sense, accompanies the maddening eccentricities of his lord. Yet Don Quixote himself is a living commentary on an abuse, i.e., overindulgence in the heady literature of romance. We may say that an event which we are forced to condemn is a comment on human life, or on the sad pass to which things have come, or on the reprehensible attitude of an unpopular government; we shall state our case humorously if we manage to stay detached, or satirically if we are disposed to attack. In each instance the situation on which we choose to comment will be far larger in range than the words devoted to it; our comment will be onesided and charged, because judgment, in order to become applicable to a fact, must first attach itself to one of its particular traits. Thus negative commentaries will always tend toward overstatement and caricature. It may also happen, on the other hand, that the speaker is so irked by the presence of an unpleasant but immutable fact that he will lose contact with the realities of the case and record only his own emotional recoil or at best a series of thrusts and jabs. Not by chance do we say, by way of praise, that a comment is pertinent, while we demand of a description that it be complete and of an explanation that it be correct.

We must add that commentaries of this kind often indicate a certain cultural malaise, a defensive attitude toward a reality felt to be insistent, meaningless, and confused. It is in periods of imminent cultural change that we find such commentaries upon the contemporary scene as Erasmus' *Praise of Folly* and Sebastian Brant's *Ship of Fools;* or, to cite a more recent example, the vogue of political cartoons in the modern world. All of these are signs of a crisis of faith, for a man who is sure of where he stands will either deliver a direct attack, forsaking the limbo of sarcastic remarks, or restate the unshaken certainty of his creed. In the latter case he will leave commentaries behind—at least the kind which we just described—in order to devote all his strength to the representation of those positive values in which he believes.

That the visual arts can produce commentary of the most damning kind goes without saying, even though the authors of such commentaries must forego the quick momentary relief which verbal comment can provide. Their range, on the other hand, is likely to be wider, for where idealization is as deeply ingrained as it is in painting, it may suffice to show things as they really are in order to record an intense emotional recoil. Thus social commentary in American art needed only to state such facts as the squalor and staleness of life in the slums to expose a society that tolerates these conditions. The same applies even more strongly to the representation of war, which need only be shown in its true cruelty to arouse the condemnation of the beholder. A striking example is Goya's series of etchings, "The Disasters of War," a grim commentary, in the form of haphazard scenes, written on the margin of an overwhelming fact. The same master's work illustrates the curious way in which a commentary, shocked by the magnitude of its topic, may lose its objective basis and retreat into the private precinct of dreams. His series "Los Caprichos" begins as a commentary on the follies of men but soon abandons contact with social facts to lose itself in oppressive nightmares teeming with devils and ghouls. One is reminded of medieval *drôlerie*, marginal comment in the strictest sense, which continuously mingles satire with the presentation of fantastic conceits.

We can now come to grips with commentaries whose mode of operation is indirect, and whose discussion we have deferred in order to get simpler matters out of the way first. In contrast to those functions which we have just described, these commentaries do not have a subject which transcends them in bulk, since there is a transposition of meaning instead of a difference of scale. There are now two subjects, one apparent, one true, of which the latter is in the background and momentarily veiled, while the former refers to it by circuitous means. The result will be a riddle, a riddle unless the true topic can be grasped instantaneously. In order to effect this and to prevent the delay that would turn such comment into a pictorial charade, topics must be chosen from notorious recent events, so that quick recognition will take place. Comments of this sort often serve as weapons in the political arena, expendable missiles that can be used only as long as their topical quality remains intact. Once the contingency has passed, their message may fall upon deaf ears and appeal to unseeing eyes. Such commentaries have an allusive bent, since they hint broadly at what remains unsaid and thus presuppose the beholder's awareness of certain current and public events. We must add that the transition from the apparent to the real subject may be made through the agency of words, which provide the key to the manner in which the image is to be read.

An Italian election poster of 1956, referring to the then recent changes in Russia, furnishes an excellent example of such commentary. It shows four pigs standing round a table, each so designed as to suggest a familiar figure in Soviet political life. The explanation of this riddle came in the words of one of these animals: "Comrades, I have a distressing revelation to make: Stalin was a pig."

I have cited this particular political cartoon because the events in question are recent enough to give full resonance to the method of attack. No contemporary will find it hard to believe that the reaction of many to the thrust was a hearty laugh, caused by the sudden shift from the apparent subject—an assembly of pigs —to a reality almost totally foreign to it. There is thus a conflict between seemingly irreconcilable worlds, which is suddenly resolved when we realize the presence of a visual metaphor: the commentator has achieved his aim the instant our understanding catches on and we gain an insight, in simplified visual terms, into a situation that had seemed paradoxical and complex.

We said of commentaries of this kind that they embody a judgment and we implied that the author, no matter how irritated and desperate, arrogates to himself an aloofness that places him above and outside the matter judged. It is an attitude hard to reconcile with the production of serious art and thus, if ingrained, it may hamper the painter in his further search: witness the recent case of George Grosz, one of the most biting commentators in the history of art, who lost all the sharpness and pungency of his style when he turned from criticizing the German bourgeois to more conventional subjects.

We may be certain, at any rate, that when an indirect subject, even one of disproportionate size, is rendered without derogatory intent, the quality of the work as commentary is weakened, while the allusive character remains intact. This is true of the grouping of visual metaphors during and after the Italian Renaissance, when sets of classical scenes were combined for the purpose of glorifying a prince. To us, who are late-born and uninformed, such works of art—e.g., Vasari's frescoes in the Palazzo Vecchio in Florence—show no more than their apparent mythological theme, and we learn with considerable surprise that they should all be read with an eye to their concealed dynastic sense. The contemporary courtier felt otherwise, for to him the allusion to the prince was bound to come first, while the apparent subjects supplied only a set of variants of an underlying theme. Therefore, no matter how diverse the scenes, he saw commentaries on the same central topic everywhere. We hasten to add that comments of this kind, which have at their core neither a judgment nor the intention to penetrate, are bound to be superficial indeed—more so, in a sense, than the airiest remarks of a conversationalist. They are flatteries meant to amplify their topic rather than to contribute toward an understanding of it. Thus, while they show how the prince's glory rebounds from the most unexpected corners of the universe, they are so external and stereotyped that they provide nothing in the way of analysis.

It is tempting to take a glance, before we close, at those kindred likenesses—another Renaissance fad—whose dependence on their subject is due to their own enigmatic and paradoxical quality. These, for once, are not commentaries in any sense, since they reveal their topic as a whole, but they, too, are subject functions, since they demand that our attention be trained upon their subjects, which thus outweigh them because they monopolize our interest. Most of these require a key to be understood, and they retain a lingering aura of depth even after comprehension has dawned, thus preventing us from resting content in the study of visual identities. We find examples of such oddities in hieroglyphic script as freely reconstructed by Renaissance minds, and in those emblems, tightly-packed combinations of visual forms, which grew out of the preoccupation with hieroglyphics. All of these are assemblies of incongruous shapes, metaphors stranded in our midst without the identifying framework that only language can provide. Their task was to render sentences by optical means. Since they held a position midway between riddles and the more accessible types of common script, their makers were advised to stay clear of both the extremes of the unintelligible and the obvious. I quote as an example the well-known printer's mark of the Aldine Press, which conveys the motto "Festina Lente"—"make haste slowly"—by the image of a mercurial dolphin twisted around an anchor.

We shall end by pointing out that illustrations, unless they secure the rank of independent and self-contained works of art, may be defined as visual commentaries upon the accompanying text, simply because their intermittent display cannot keep pace with the continuity of the written word. Dominion over the book or the page will almost always go to the text, which will secure for itself a maximum of unbroken expanse, while illustrations will have to fit themselves in where best they can, either in the margins or in odd spaces saved out between the lines. Any illustration that defies this dependence upon its environment, either by a heavy frame or because its formal organization is complete in itself, will by that very fact transcend the humble function accorded to it and cease to be a true sample of its kind. Illustrations are thus commentaries made visually manifest. It is not surprising to find that their range, like that of their linguistic next-of-kin, extends from objective interpretations of the text to fantasies, some of them very personal indeed, engendered by the author's words in the mind of the illustrator. In either case, if they are worthy of their name, they will depend on the text for that authentication which other likenesses find in themselves. When we say that a painting is illustrative—even though there are no words to be read alongside—we mean that it fails to attain complete unity of form and that this weakness, often caused by a plethora of detail, would be justified only if there were a visible dependence upon a text. Here the logical deficiency which we found lurking in all subject functions and which establishes their inferiority to their principals, becomes a criterion of style.

XIII *Substitution in Art*

To most of us the doctrine that art may serve substitutional ends has a rather disagreeable sound, since cultural habit has accustomed us to think of it as an activity too noble to be degraded by subservience. We shall not try to discourage this sentiment. But let the reader ask himself whether he has never debased art by using it as a makeshift or stopgap and he is likely to find that he has some rather awkward confessions to make. What else is it but substitution when we employ art as a means of escape, putting it in the place of the high adventure, the sensuous repose, the riches and satisfactions that life has failed to provide for us? And how many of us could assert, without perjuring ourselves, that we have never sought the vicarious stimulus of the movie house, of detective fiction, and of the soap opera? Representations in these fields of work are created for the express purpose of providing a short but effective escape from the mechanical routine of modern life; and the existence of enormous amusement industries proves that there must be substitutes for repressed human needs if the machinery of our civilization is not to grind to a stop.

How disastrous the effect can be when secondary diversions take the place of reality need hardly be emphasized, for we see all about us the loss of inner wealth, the inability to taste the savor of things that comes from acceptance of experience in terms of manufactured substitute capsules. Nor can it be denied that there is a specific substitutional art, created with the weary city-dweller in mind and distinguished not only by the predominance of certain media such as those of television and of the cinema but also by specific artistic attitudes. Since it is the call for experience that is to be met, we find a pronounced emphasis upon suspense as a means of increasing the thrill of momentary escape, and a strong use of empathy to pull the observer into the plot as if his own fate depended upon that of the protagonist. Thus when the spectator leaves the place where such experience is purveyed, still panting with the excitement he has gone through, he will be forced to confess that, as long as the incantation lasted, he had been effectively transposed into another life.

It will be noted that the ability to produce sensations of this kind is mostly limited to the temporal arts, since they alone are able to accumulate emotional strain in the beholder. There is, however, one way in which the modern world employs the visual arts for substitutional aims: what we call advertisement is based upon the notion that existing drives for possession can be fanned and channelled by displaying the images of

objects whose purchase, so we are told, will assuage
desire. Thus the likeness acts as a guide toward satisfactions painted in glowing terms, just as a mental
image sharpens a drive by providing it with an intermediate goal. Advertisements are images in the public
domain, designed to exploit the mechanism of man's
volitional life for commercial ends. We need hardly
state that because they are meant to lead us on by
turning us into acquisitive machines guided by the conditioned reflexes appropriate to a customer's station
in life, they do not truly replace what they depict lest
they defeat their own aims. Thus they differ from mental
images, which as creations of our own inner life are
able to close in upon us whenever we lose conscious control. A similar divergence exists between them and escape art, in that the latter, since it provides us with
correlatives of often unconscious drives, may not be
recognized for what it is. Designed to remedy the sense
of emptiness that is the curse of modern man, it calms
his cravings by providing experiences whose substitute
character remains concealed. For that very reason no
exposure to escape art can bring more than passing
relief, so that other exposures will soon be needed to
dull the resurgent pain.

There is, on the other hand, a kinship of the most
obvious sort between advertisement and propaganda art,
except that the latter, instead of depicting its subject
in the rosiest light, may be called upon to brutalize and
distort it in order to arouse. It may then be said that
propaganda art substitutes for the adversary as he
really is a likeness whose provocative slant is so strong
that the truth cannot prevail against the image put in
its place. In either case the likeness is meant to induce
action of a specific kind by sharpening a potential feel-

ing into a drive toward its referent. When thus employed as a mere correlative of a drive, as something that is meant either to entice or to inspire revulsion, art loses its relationship to the objective order of things and thus fails to make values manifest. Instead of interpreting its subject, it merely presents superficial features designed to bring about the desired psychological effect.

Thus our analysis confirms what one might reasonably expect after what we said earlier about the character of adaptive substitutes: namely, that in advertising, propaganda, and substitutional art generally the function which we assigned to mental images and dreams is continued into the world of waking experiences, except that the selection of images put before our mind, instead of being controlled from within and in a manner harmonious with our organic needs, is now in the hands of persons who may make irresponsible use of their chance to play upon our faculties. It is certain, at any rate, that the substitutions we have dealt with up to now are of a primitive kind, mere extensions into the framework of social life of the polyphony of instinctual utterances. As yet we are not very far from magic, i.e., the mistaken belief that images, instead of merely stimulating us to action, have a direct effect upon the object toward which such action tends.

We shall deal briefly with what may be called substitutes *in loco*, likenesses which appear at the place where their referent should have been. Their usual task is to deceive, and they become mere lies or hollow pretense as soon as their claim has been exposed. For the material which has a rightful share in any truly representational work of art has here been used only as a means to an end, which is meant to disappear in the

intended effect, so that it becomes a reminder of the
failure of a fraudulent scheme once the illusion has collapsed. But although questionable and wrought without
true artistic intent, substitutional effigies hold a certain
place in the history of art. They were, for example, a
means of preserving the fast-waning shape of the dead,
before it had begun to disintegrate. In this capacity,
they played a role in Roman funerary rites, which lasted
too long to permit a continuous exposure of the deceased. Such substitutes *in loco* became works of art
when the funerary effigies were turned into portraits
realistically conceived. An even more striking case of
the influence of such substitution upon the plastic arts
is found in the tomb statues of ancient Egypt, which
were meant to serve the soul as a habitat after it had
been wrenched by death from the body that had been
its former seat. Because of their purpose, these statues
display a precocious love of realistic form, required to
make sure that the soul, instead of fluttering about,
would recognize the body to which it had once belonged.
Thus the functions of such effigies may be vital enough:
they are part of man's unavailing defense against the
flux of time, a pathetic effort to prolong individual life
beyond the barrier of death.

These effigies differ from the substitutes discussed
before in that they are used as a means to satisfy a
specific desire. Escape art and advertisement, on the
other hand, corresponding as they do to rather broad
and general drives, have much wider fields open to them.
The desires to which they cater can find fulfillment in
anything that lies within their scope; which means, since
escape art deals out "experience" in the broadest sense,
that almost the entire range of human life, in all its
complexity, falls under its purview.

We turn now to those substitutional events that are not correlatives of a drive but of clear-cut individualized interests. Whereas our drives cater to human needs and thus are linked with a self-centered system of co-ordinates, our conscious attention tends to focus upon specific things and their immediate value and distinctiveness; there is, therefore, an outward projection of emphasis when instinctual indifference to reality gives way to an appreciation of things for their own sake. And this change of accent seems to be accompanied by a change of consciousness, for once the object is allowed to assert itself, there can be no more of that vagueness of latent tendencies which we found to underlie the satisfaction of drives, since mental concentration demands control and intentness. It would seem certain, on the other hand, that attention cannot be sustained unless propelled by desire, which gives it its power and intensity; and that it may thus easily lapse, giving way to a more primitive egocentric state, as soon as we have exhausted our capacity to concentrate.

With these few words for a guide we can now see what state of mind is required by those substitute likenesses which stand for individual entities. All of these presuppose on our part a degree of conscious intent not demanded by the mere correlatives of drives. And since it is now the interpretant who holds the reins instead of being the dupe of outsiders playing upon his frustrated faculties, there will be no more manipulation of latent appetites as practiced by the purveyors of amusement and propaganda. The beholder will be sufficiently aware of his own turn of interest to go out and seek the sources of vicarious experience. And another change will follow from this: although escape art is able to present itself as an aesthetic experience free from substitutional ties and afterthoughts, this dissimulation of purpose will have to cease when likenesses minister to specific desires. There will always be a shadowy reference to a principal, even though little is known about its structure and identity. Thus when we avail ourselves of a map to substitute for the experience of an unexplored countryside, we do so knowing in advance what area it is that holds our interest; whereas the same map, as a mere representation of a tract of land, and approached without the assumption of practical interest, will require no such advance knowledge of identities. There is a striking similarity to subject functions, which, like the substitutes with which we are now concerned, are rudderless unless kept on an even keel by a steady glance at their principal. We will not be surprised to find that both descriptions and explanatory designs such as charts and diagrams may not only render their subject in their own peculiar ways, but also put themselves in its place if the subject is not otherwise accessible.

There is one more indirect consequence which, this time, follows from the nature of substitutes. Substitutional imagery is limited to a context of fact, excluding that relation to the realm of imaginable possibilities which is the privilege of other likenesses. Such images must find their place within the real world and thus within the dimensions of space and time. Instead of existing in that Platonic universe where subjects have their being when freely conceived, the referents of substitutional imagery will have to be material and concrete, no matter in what context they may be placed. While a statue may *represent* St. Peter as an entity in our thoughts, of whose place in history we are well aware, it can *substitute* only for St. Peter as a living individual, who is now experienced as reaching across into our world. What is true of this particular case applies to substitute imagery of any kind, including the systems of theological conceits which decorate churches and temple walls. It is only a natural consequence of this that substitutional likenesses tend, at least on the more primitive levels of thought, to be carriers of real energy, intermediaries in the magic sense of bringing an essence close to us. On the other hand, if the subject of a likeness comes out of the crucible of the human mind—say a dragon or some other fantastic beast—its substitutional character can be retained only if we think up a subterfuge that will give it citizenship in the real world. Our fantastic beast will thus have to live in some distant enchanted woods, or it may find itself styled as the inhabitant of a psychological or historic universe, e.g., as "the idea of a dragon according to Medieval belief" or as "the creature that occurred in last night's dream."

The limits put upon art by its substitutional use are thus severe and restrictive. No likeness can be a makeshift—assuming it is not a mere correlative of a drive —unless it is supported by explicit belief. Skepticism will act as a destructive force and the only way in which a subject can be retained after its reality has been disproved is by letting it retreat into its ideal Platonic world. The importance of this limitation will come home to us when we realize, as will be explained further on, how broad is the vicarious function of art; that all likenesses which serve educational, commemorative, and religious aims, as well as many others, are substitutional to some degree; and that therefore a vast part of man's output of imagery—the part that is most necessary and vital to him—requires prior confidence in its credibility. It is perhaps no exaggeration to say that the cultural output of any human group may be divided into products which presuppose such trust, because they substitute for unavailable aspects of the world, and products which can be freely conceived, because they have no substitutional aim; with the proviso, we must repeat, that likenesses which act as substitutes must always stand for vaguely-known entities in some kind of real universe.

With this condition in mind we can now state under what conditions a likeness can act as a makeshift or substitute. The condition is simply this: that there must be a principal important to us but so difficult to attain by direct means that its remoteness compels us to fall back upon a likeness which is available and close by. There is thus a gradation of values so arranged that, while the referent will be preponderant, the substitute will be given preference because it is present, instrumental, and ready for use. It will matter little whether the principal is beyond our reach permanently or temporarily, or whether its unavailability is due to its distance, its complexity, or to a combination of both. Thus substitution, here as at all other times, is essentially a practical device designed to bring the remote and cumbersome within mental range. The replacement of a region by a map, of a musical performance by its score, of an area of knowledge by a textbook presenting it in survey form, are all dictated by utilitarian needs. Our mode of action implies in each case that it is more feasible, at the moment at least, to deal with the substitute than to try to explore its inaccessible prototype.

The need for a substitute becomes acute when the entity represented is so menacing but diffuse that the only means of domesticating it consists of bringing it to concrete sensory evidence. We spoke in our first chapter of the modern attempt to explain the rise of representation in art—in its post-paleolithic form—as a means of defense against the seemingly inexorable powers of the unseen. We can now restate this etiological theory in our own terms and say that the task of protecting man's nakedness against spiritual threats was at first undertaken by substitutional means: vague demons were compelled to declare themselves and thus rendered innocuous by replacing them with their images in stone or paint. By laying this snare against the spectral powers, man pulled them within his own sphere of influence and thereby gained ascendance over them.

A second and more constructive defense was also effected by substitutional means. In order to surround himself with a protective sense of order and of measurement, man prepared an abbreviated image of the universe—in the form of sacred architecture and its cosmic imagery—as a screen against the turbulent assault of the unknown. He thereby gained a great stabilizing influence, for, however erroneous his view of reality, the very fact that he dared to represent—and thus to make available—the missing aspects of the world enlarged his area of safety. Instead of being the victim of chaotic fears, constantly threatened by entities closing in on him, he now possessed a substitute universe of his own so arranged that by ritual action within it he could limit the area of the unforeseen. We will realize the significance of this creation of a cosmic framework by substitutional means when we consider that its psychological basis is found in the experience of all: every man, today as in the past, depends for the confidence and security he needs on the belief that there is a world beyond the present scene on whose order and continuity he can rely. This sense of a total environment is in fact an a priori condition of experience. If it is abridged, then, like primitive man, we feel pressed and pursued;

in the extreme case, we become the victims of an anxiety which may lead us to the psychiatric ward.

It was thus the achievement of early man to have translated feelings common to us all into concrete and visible terms. The imagery of temples and holy places all over the world is meant to give a comprehensive likeness of heaven and earth, of the powers that rule them and human life, and of the periodicity of nature in their keep. Architecture provides the symbolic frame within which the constituent parts of the universe have their appointed place; and by orienting the structure in accordance with the movement of the heavenly bodies this vicarious totality is made to coincide with and therefore —according to the mode of reasoning of archaic thought —to act upon the greater totality of which it is part. In such buildings pictorial substitution may be practiced on a momentous scale. And no wonder, for they—or at least their interiors—often achieve a sense of isolation so complete as to keep all environmental influences at bay. By thus shutting out human affairs and all their inconsequential noise an opportunity is gained to let the larger aspects of the world gain the upper hand. These will be shown by representational means in order to provide a worthy frame in which the gods may appear. Again we can cite a situation in individual experience which furnishes a parallel to and perhaps an explanation of the practice concerned. The state of "brown study," which many of us know, finds us alone, remote, dedicated, and bent upon a lighted page; the happiness of this concentrated frame of mind is due at least in part to the sense of an adumbrated world in the surrounding dark, a world, however distant and vague, with whose parts the reader is in sympathetic touch.

It is then the hallmark of religious art that it supplements the range of our immediate concerns with images of remote and inaccessible things—things which it brings close to us by endowing them with exalted but familiar shapes. Indeed, by far the better part of man's artistic output has been dedicated to the exploration, often by imaginative means, of those aspects of the world that are transcendant or distant in space and in time and which are thus either difficult of access or altogether beyond our reach. To the religious subjects which provide a framework shared by all must be added the records of persons and events from the past and likenesses which are merely meant to provide information about unavailable objects of all kinds. Many of these are substitutional in the strictest sense: when we erect a monument to the memory of an important man, when we let a statue take the place of a saint, when we examine a picture instead of the phenomenon depicted in it, we are in a substitutional frame of mind. And it may be regarded as an indirect confirmation of this that substitution may easily shade into identity, in which case the image holds the field alone instead of sharing it with the primary reality it represents. Thus, particularly if political passions are involved, a statue may become the person of which it is a likeness, and hatred against an oppressive regime may be expressed by overturning the image of the ruler. Whenever we act upon a likeness instead of merely contemplating it there is always this chance that both substitution and representation may be eclipsed.

It must not be believed, on the other hand, that all those likenesses which represent distant and inaccessible things were intended only for substitutional ends. We have experienced an emancipation from servitude which we owe primarily to the Greeks. And it has been possible ever since to render a mythological or religious scene merely because it appeals to us for its own sake. All that is required of us is that the purpose which the likeness might serve, commemorative, liturgical, or mystical, be expunged and that instead there be the corresponding context of thought.

Man's immediate environment has only rarely been an accepted subject of art. When this happened, as it did early in China and again recently in the Western world, the reason may have been a naïve satisfaction with man's earthly life and a corresponding unreadiness to venture into the unknown. Or perhaps we should attribute such an abandonment of a world-wide tradition to the practice of *l'art pour l'art,* for which any motif will suffice provided it offers substantial fare to the artist's eye. There is a correlation which may not be due to chance between "factualism" in art and the prevalence of exclusively aesthetic attitudes.

As far as the awareness of substitution is concerned, it will vary according to the extent to which the beholder is cognizant of his own motivation. Pre-eminence will go to the likeness itself; its sensory presence will suffice to establish its primacy over secondary attitudes. If the mind is to discover its own substitutional bent, it must thus turn upon itself and engage in introspective techniques. Where there is no self-knowledge, as in the case of the average customer of the amusement industries, there is also no sense of the presence of a substitutional device. The worshipper, on the other hand, when prostrated before an image of his god, may find it easy to recognize its vicariousness because he knows of the longing that brought him there and thus of the mainspring of his own attitudes.

There is another factor which influences us. All substitution, if it is part of cultural life, has a dual aspect: one communal and objective, consisting of the preparations made to present the public with materials in manageable vicarious shape; the other private and subjective and composed of the attitudes we take toward this offer of useful commodities. We believe that full consciousness of substitution cannot come to pass unless both aspects are made to co-operate.

The social factor pervades all our intellectual life. When we draw a map, write a textbook, or give an academic course, we provide a transcript, in systematic form, of the labors—thoughts, measurements, and experiments—undertaken by past workers in the field. By thus correlating the knowledge that exists we enable our listeners to begin where other minds have left off, rather than to pit their inadequate strength against mountains of undigested facts. We substitute, in other words, our over-all treatment of the theme for the many contributions, large and small, that have been made in the past, and thus enable our audience to avail itself of materials too scattered to be picked up piecemeal. It is one of the merits of representational techniques that they allow this telescoping of pertinent facts, while eliminating others, and that they thus fit a likeness for its career of social usefulness. We may say, therefore, that the devices by which a civilization transmits its inheritance to the future have a strong tinge of vicariousness.

A sense of caution prevents us, on the other hand, from attributing to most of these cultural tools a completely substitutional purpose, since our chief witness, the interpretant, refuses to come to our aid. The only way to convince him would be to show that books, maps, and lectures, while they instruct, also liberate him from those labors which he would have to perform if he tried to reach his intellectual goal by his own unaided strength; and that, therefore, they substitute for tasks that he has been spared. We may, for instance, point out to him that by using a map he escapes having to go out, as the surveyors did, and taking all the necessary measurements on the spot.

He is likely to answer, if he knows his own mind, that his intention is not to duplicate measurements, as if these were desirable in themselves, but to learn about the lay of the land and perhaps to prepare a trip; and that therefore there is no correspondence between his drive, which aims at objectives of a practical kind, and the operations required to make a map. Finally, and here we come to the core of his thought, substitution, in order to be complete, calls for the activation of one single drive which will envelop both substitute and referent and thus lead to an equivalence of activities. Clearly, if these criteria are to apply, then we can concede only a limited substitutional role to the means of communication which we have discussed, since all of these are merely subservient to a drive which exceeds and surpasses them. If the interpretant is to be aware of the substitution that is taking place, then representation must stand for the means by which knowledge has been obtained, for instance when an account of an experiment is accepted as a substitute for a similar experiment which the reader has to forego because of lack of skill or opportunity.

Many other substitutional types conform to the sharpened criteria which we just pronounced. Our reading, for instance, of a musical score, instead of attending a concert performance, is a makeshift procedure and

we experience it as such, for both the evening at home
and the one in the concert hall are correlatives of the
same desire. Even if there is no performance to which
we could have gone, some consciousness of substitution
may persist, though our drive must then be turned
toward an imaginary concert which did not take place.
Complete substitution also occurs when we study the
portrait of a deceased individual in an attempt to recapture some inkling of his living presence—the very
experience for the sake of which the majority of portraits were made.

A special place must be given to those symbols and
effigies which are at the service of a religious cult, for
all of these have a presubstitutional phase that precedes their use as vicarious entities. A legitimate method
of approaching them consists of assuming that they
stand for and in place of their respective gods and thus
are truly substitutional. The worshipper, aware of their
vicariousness, will then use them as tools that will provide him with a glimpse that is equivalent, though inferior, to being face to face with a recondite and essentially inapproachable divinity. The idol and the god
whom it represents will partake of the same drive, and
thus will enter into a relation of ritual equivalence. The
worshipper, in turn, will be able to claim, if he has
heard of the strictures of Jewish and Christian divines,
that he has kept veneration within bounds and avoided
the pitfalls of idolatry.

There is, however, an older, more basic approach,
for which the image is more than a spiritual tool within
a substitutional frame. According to that attitude, the
image itself is charged with divinity. It is alive and
aflame with the entity which it represents. Thus it cannot be a makeshift for what constitutes its very core.

Since this spectral charge is viewed as a quality which the image contains, whoever possesses the required technique can release its force for his own benefit. We speak then of the magical use of art. It is an indication of beginning rationality when this original identity is turned into the relation of an intermediary to its outer correlates, with the effect that the likeness, in transmitting the sacred essence, acts like a transformer in an electric circuit: a means to adapt the current generated in the powerhouse to the requirements of local use. It will then be believed that the god reaches through the likeness toward us, just as we try to reach toward him through the same intermediary, whose function is that of a sacramental tool through which the divinity communicates himself to us.

We have emphasized the existence of a presubstitutional phase in order to highlight the change that must have occurred when the next stage of development was reached. As long as the theory of the charged image prevailed, there was little concern with verisimilitude. The divinity could be housed in a sacred stone, a fetish, or an idol possessing few recognizable traits. Since it was the power within the object that ruled, no clear distinction needed to be made between a primary thing— a tree or a rock—and one that had been carved into representational shape. There must have been a decisive shift when the god began to dissociate himself from his abode, taking its power to himself and leaving it stranded as a substitute. At that moment the fetish was deprived of its life. It became possible to charge, as was done by several writers of the Old Testament, that any effort to localize the divine was an example of a materialistic heresy, of a delusion that identified God with a mere piece of wood or of stone. But another conclusion could be drawn from this: granted that the image had lost most of its potency, was it not then the artist's task to supply the reality that had fled from it by embodying it vicariously in visual forms? Now that the divine substance had been withdrawn, could one not try to make up for the loss by creating its semblance in artistic terms? We believe, in other words, that at the moment when the image had lost its charge, it gained its emancipation as a work of art, and that this visual birth occurred precisely because the status of the image as a substitute could not provide satisfaction in itself.

If our speculation is correct, then the idol would have a tendency to fall behind the development of more substitutional forms of art. We would then expect it to retain its primitive shape at times when other likenesses had long progressed toward more realistic forms. And we would anticipate that the lead in the early development of art would fall to other types such as dynastic imagery, memorial statuary, and the accessories of tombs, all of which are more likely to be conceived in substitutional terms than are the idols and symbols of the cult. Within the religious orbit we would expect that the cosmic environment of the god and the mythological exploits which he performed would precede the idol into the new realistic world, because these subjects had a weaker magical force and therefore could be transformed more readily. It is possible that the subsequent evolution of the idol in its turn shows a retroactive effect from its field of expansion in the decoration of the temple walls, on the assumption that the god himself had become part of the universe which he helped to rule. The transition from the fetish to the realistic image of later times would then be due to the incipient conception of the world as an orderly totality, within which the god held a circumscribed, although dominant, place.

We must put an end to this speculative strain, lest it carry us too far from our analytic task. Suffice it to state our belief that detailed research in the early art of Greece, India, and the ancient Near East will confirm the suggestions we have put forward.

We shall conclude by pointing out that substitutes *in loco*, as we have called them, had a prerealistic phase during which there seems to have been a strong belief in magic identities. The death mask may well have originated as a device for imparting continued life to the deceased. We are not the first to suggest that the change from its originally rigid and impersonal forms to the realism of Roman portrait art was due to a loss of faith in its efficacy as a tool, which turned a magic preservative into a visual substitute.

XIV *Similarity and Recognition*

It is difficult to speak of similarity, essential
though it is to mimetic representation as a link that
connects a likeness with its principal. In an earlier chapter we described similarity as the common basis of
representation, a necessary ingredient without which
neither the creation nor the experience of representation
would come to pass. But once we ask what similarity is,
how it is defined and how it is recognized in an individual
case, we will find ourselves at sea, for the phenomenon
is so basic to our understanding of the world, so deeply
ingrained in every perceptual and cognitive act, that
we can only point it out, knowing that we shall be immediately understood. The questions of what constitutes resemblance to a given subject, how far it can
be stretched, and what are the variations of its acceptance among men, can hardly be stated in general terms.

Only empirical research will be useful here. What laws there may be in this much neglected domain are likely to be accessible only to a revised method of Gestalt analysis, modeled upon the work that has been done in the investigation of abstract configurations in the visual field. Our own essentially phenomenological approach will not do.

Since, therefore, this aspect of the theme is in many ways beyond our scope, we will have to restrict our discussion to those features which lend themselves to treatment in general terms. We shall start by stating that resemblance in the visual arts has a much narrower range than similarity in the universe at large. As experienced in our dealings with the outer world, resemblance cuts freely across the classifications of things. A mountain resembles a castle or a cloud, a person's face that of a species of animal, a color possesses definite but enigmatic links with corresponding sensations of sound and tactile sensibility. The more we let our spontaneous imagination roam, the more we become aware of these expressive affinities which make strange bed-fellows of heterogeneous things. They constitute the rock-bottom of visual experience, the first and most primitive knowledge of the world that precedes all later forms of insight. Such physiognomic relations were invoked in the creation and application of words, which are apt to fit a number of analogous referents as long as their meaning has not been expressly defined. We can speak of something as brilliant or obscure or hard in the context of several sensory fields without unduly stretching the meaning of these words; and it thus seems likely that the original application of many terms comprised this ambiguity toward their referents. Metaphors, if our reasoning is right, did not originate as the conscious transfer of meaning from one sphere to another; they reflect, rather, a fund of related experiences so closely akin that their common expressive characteristics outweigh their differences in logical terms. Much the same conclusion is suggested by the fact that the possible usage of a word, i.e., its range of meaning, can be defined only by enumerating the various contexts in which it may appear.

The reader will notice that this multiple meaning of words is the precise inverse of what happens in the representational arts, where the principal is one while its possible representatives are many. This fact alone should suffice to suggest that the proliferation of analogies which we found to exist in the verbal realm has no counterpart in the representational field. Indeed, what is characteristic of words is an exception in the visual arts, where resemblance always remains beholden to the subject and its place in the scheme of things. We can only represent a tree by the likeness of one, and a lion only by the image of such a quadruped. If there is a change in the category to which the likeness belongs, this change involves relations within the same logical sphere rather than transposition to another one. (The only exceptions to this rule are certain visual metaphors of which we shall speak later on.) It is possible, for instance, to represent an individual by the generalized likeness of his class, and the class by a category of still broader scope—techniques commonly used in all archaic phases of art. The only condition that must be observed is that, as we rise in the logical scale, the visual construction must remain the same. We can, as we said, represent a lion by the vaguer likeness of a somewhat featureless quadruped. But when it comes to man, with his upright stance, the only regression that is permissible consists of passing from the individual to the class and ultimately to the race, since any image of still more general scope would confound man with creatures walking on all fours. Another slight infraction of the rule of representational faithfulness consists of the well-known and useful artistic trick of representing a whole by its parts—an invaluable device in the painter's and sculptor's hands for clarifying what he set out to show and eliminating unessential details. Thus it is possible to represent a forest by a tree, an army by a few of the soldiers that form part of it, or a person by the features of his face. But again, as in the previous case, the relation between subject and likeness is very close, showing little of that spontaneity which characterizes our perception of resemblances among the phenomena of reality.

The question thus obtrudes itself: What is it in representation that prevents the unchecked proliferation of analogies? We can give a very simple answer: the limitation springs from the demands of the representational rationale, which insists that likenesses present aspects or projections of a given subject and thus cuts short the range of permissible similarity. By making each group of images depend upon one subject instead of abandoning it to the reign of uncontrolled association, the rationale brings order and reason into an otherwise only loosely-organized field. Its role is the same as in categorical and legal representation, domains which owe their firmness of structure to the steadying influence of their rationale. Our mind would let both common essence and community of interest exceed all acceptable bonds, if their flow were not checked by limiting factors, in the first case by the relation of the part to the whole, in the second by that of a person to his possible legal representatives.

It cannot be argued against this that the existence of double images in art disproves the adherence of any given likeness to a single referent. It is true that such images present configurations which call for interpretations in a two-fold sense. But a close analysis will always show that they are concretions of two separate subjects projected upon the same sensory field. They consist of two images so superimposed that they encounter each other where they coincide—one of them dominant and detailed, the other suggested by fragmentary means. Thus, for instance, in Arcimboldo's painting of "Summer," lettuces, cabbages, and fruit combine to create a conglomerate image of a human head. But it is not so much the vegetables themselves which form the constituents of the resurgent shape, as certain chosen areas and lines, points of visual support so placed that they will congeal into the adumbrated likeness of a man. Thus, instead of one image charged with the task of conveying two separate ideas simultaneously, we have two images rolled into one.

The same applies to pictures which are so arranged that the primary likeness and its competitive ghost are of approximately the same size, so that the eye, instead of climbing from the smaller to the larger shape, discovers both within the total configuration itself. This is the case when the contour of a hill is to be experienced also as a human face. But whereas in beholding one of Arcimboldo's heads both identities are grasped with very little delay, this is not so in the latter case. It now becomes almost impossible for the mind to retain both resemblances at once, so that one interpretation will have to be suppressed while the other is temporarily paramount. Such images are disturbing to behold because memory insists upon both disjunctive views, whereas perception records only one at a time, with the thoroughly unpleasant result that our faculties seem to be at odds. It cannot be claimed, at any rate, that representation itself has been split in two, since our experience records two successive and separate views.

Finally, if the artist proceeds to show two competing forms simultaneously, letting one of them end where the other begins, the logical situation is altogether changed. What is now presented to the interpretant's glance is simply one complex being so composed that it will possess several complementary identities. Thus representation does no more than record a transformation that has taken place—the previous genesis, in the artist's mind, of a complex image. We do not believe that those surrealists are right who claim to catch the birth of the image in its track, letting both ideation and representation coalesce into one single mental act. There must always be a choice, although a repeated one perhaps, between the spontaneous expression of an impulse from within and the always deliberate act of producing a likeness of an inner event.

That double images are composed of very primitive stuff, and thus come from that very matrix of thought out of which the figurative meaning of words is made, can hardly be open to debate. The fact that they always tend to give a physiognomic interpretation of things, changing them into faces and threatening masks, would be sufficient in itself to place them rather low on the psychological scale. In addition, the presence of competing identities, well-known from the observation of dreams, links them with primary processes of the mind.

While acknowledging this, we only claim that when double images, however erratic and refractory, are caught in the medium of art, they are compelled to abide by the same law of representational fidelity which holds for all other likenesses.

What we called visual metaphors in art differ from double images in that here the likeness, though unambiguous and complete, invites us to treat it in analogical terms. Thus the relation between it and its principal is not based on visual equivocation but on an analogy which involves a similarity of attributes in both the entity portrayed and the one to which it refers. The representation of the Good Shepherd in art is thus an indirect representation of Christ, because both the shepherd and the Divine keeper of souls hold a benign watch over their flock; a sheep, in the same period of Christian art, can also represent Christ as the Passover lamb, or human souls that have gone astray, the analogy being obvious in either case. The relation of such symbols to metaphors is confirmed by the fact that they existed in the Gospel text even before they appeared in the visual arts. But they are metaphors of a particular kind, no longer the unpremeditated result of the expressive range of words but the outcome of a deliberate choice, similes meant to illuminate an article of the creed. No wonder, therefore, that it is possible to translate their message into pictorial or sculptural terms, so that there is a stringent correspondence between the visual data and the aspect of divinity they are intended to convey.

We return once more to the realm of basic human experience, in order to stress the well-known fact that visual metaphors prevail in our impressions of our environment, both natural and artistic. Lines and colors possess a figurative charge that is no less potent because their effect upon us precedes any effort at verbal description. A color may be hard, cool, or remote, a line aspiring or depressed, whether or not these qualities become expressly articulate. The ordinary use of these "tertiary" qualities consists of putting them at the service of an aesthetic aim. Thus if our purpose is to create a representational work of art, we will let them partake in the interpretation we intend to convey. Lines and colors are then received as parts of the objects to which they adhere, so that their tertiary qualities will turn into attributes of the subject portrayed. A harmonization of implications will occur, possible only since all metaphors are endowed with multiple significance, and thus are capable of being moulded into mutual conformity. To what extent this attuning of connotations has taken place is a measure of the rank held by a work of art. Since tertiary qualities are experienced as vehicles of universals made concrete, we may say that when they share in the building of a representational work of art they function as the link between it and the expanded content it is to convey. They help the work of art to transcend its status as a mere particular and to rise to a more extended significance. And since they function, in turn, as exponents of events in that central region of the mind where exchanges of sense implications take place—events as elementary as they are indeterminate—we discover that deep strata of our person are being stirred, while our intellect is called upon to ascend to the realization of a general "truth." The comprehensive effect of outstanding works of art seems to be due to this concerted double impact upon our sensibilities.

A special case is that of those modern works of art, particularly those with a futurist slant, for which the metaphor is not only an aesthetic tool designed to bring artistic implications to light—a thing as self-effacing as it is dominant—but a topic with its own conspicuous logical rights. In this case the motif and its formal qualities tend to coincide. The result of this fusion is a new type of art that is both subjective and abstract, since things, if they are allowed to survive at all, must fight for their lives, lest they be carried away by the surrounding cascade of turbulent sensations. What general implications will be found will therefore also be of a subjective kind and will tend to coalesce with the topic as stated or conceived in advance. The subjects of such creations are the perception of speed, the feeling of being part of a crowd, or the felt trajectory of a bird in space, all of them so full of movement tingling upon our nerves that they are not likely to leave much room for the recording of ordinary visual fact. It takes some effort to remind oneself that such works of art, however vertiginous, are intended to carry a full representational load, and that what would seem a violent aberration from the norm is an effort to conquer uncharted fields for the domain of representational art. But they are evasive renditions, for apart from the strong sensations they cause, and the corresponding adumbrated sense of their intended import, they contain very little to suggest their representational role, let alone what they are meant to convey. There is, in short, a dearth of cognitive signs, as is natural in this world of colored vectors and impulses, which may force us to rely on external labels if we are to learn what had been the topic portrayed. This is a situation not unlike that of diagrams and graphs, which also refuse to reveal their representational role unless there is an explanatory inscription. Obviously, as these examples show, no analy-

sis of resemblance in art is complete unless it includes
an attempt to weigh the particular function of diacritical marks.

Let us start, as we approach this aspect of the problem, by stating that the recognition of objects in the
outer world is normally based on their expressive and
configurational charge. We know with a directness which
no challenge can shake that a face or a landscape are
familiar to us, and if we are asked why we feel so sure
we can do no more than to restate our belief—our conviction is so deeply ingrained that it defies analysis. And
we are right, for individuality, as a unique configuration of related and interdependent elements, will reveal
itself only if we are ready to weigh the interplay of its
features in its totality. The only approach that yields
direct results is the acceptance of appearance unanalyzed, the conviction that we can trust the unsolicited
self-disclosure of visual fact. And while particulars are
less highly organized, and thus admit the intrusion of
cognitive signs, they may rely upon an even deeper
memory trace for direct and instantaneous recognition.

Now assume that this method of acquiring knowledge fails, because either the phenomenon or the resources we bring to it are too indistinct to permit the
establishing of familiarity. It will then be necessary to
assure recognition by other supplementary means; we
resort to the observation of known isolated traits, and
if this does not yield the desired result, we will turn to
outward signs capable of leading us on to a coveted identity. Thus as the mutual replacement of signs proceeds,
there is a noticeable trend away from the object of our
interest and outward toward its periphery. If we cannot obtain the ideal case of recognition by physiognomic

means, then a birthmark or some other circumscribed
characteristic will have to do instead. Failing that we
may try our luck with labels, the placing of flowers in
buttonholes, or the addition of some other signal to the
body concerned. If even devices of this kind are unavailable to us, we may fall back, as a last resort, upon
environmental hints at increasing distances from the
object signified. But also, as the sign becomes more and
more remote, there is a corresponding loss of assurance
that its message will be correctly understood.

We need hardly insist that such signs can never
serve in a primary capacity, since it is very easy to
show that their operation depends upon the prior existence of physiognomic fact. Once we admit that, in
order to function as a sign, a thing must be acknowledged as having this capacity, we are forced to concede that the process requires the use of subsidiary
signs, which must be authenticated in turn, and so *ad
infinitum* beyond the limits of reason and feasibility.
There is here an interminable regression which is impossible to stop unless we recognize that at some point
the semantic function must be built upon the bedrock
of expressive fact. No wonder that as soon as their
work is done, all such signs dissolve into the physiognomic entities out of which they have come.

A further limitation of diacritical signs consists of
the fact that, unless aided by their context, they can
only point to particulars, characterizing them as members of their class, and never to a full-fledged individual.
They will serve as signs of generic qualities, functioning
variously as badges, labels, check-marks, and attributes,
pluralistic entities designed to lift a category of things
out of a welter of other entities. If there is a multipli-
cation of such signs, they will only form subcategories,

refining and differentiating them until a whole system of classification has evolved. The reason for this is plain enough, for if we distinguish an object by a diacritical mark, we will merely have made it a member of a class set off by the presence of that diacritical mark. We will have made no declaration about its innate qualities; and while the discovery of individuality may follow suit, it will not be a consequence of the cognitive process that has taken place.

If we are to break through the defences which the individual puts up against this kind of indirect cognitive attack, we shall have to strengthen the evidence of diacritical marks by the affirmation of corroborating circumstance. It will not suffice, for instance, to agree that an unknown newcomer will be marked by a red feather on his hat. Unless it is also understood where and when the meeting with him is to take place—say, at a given station and at the arrival of a certain train from New York—we may commit the silly mistake of regarding anybody anywhere in the world as our expected friend provided he wears a red feather on his hat. The case is clear enough to be readily generalized, and we shall therefore limit ourselves to pointing out that even if a landmark is immobile and reliably known, it will serve as a cognitive sign only if the circumstances of the approach are such as to bear out its claim. If we saw the towers of Chartres in the American West, we would have the choice of concluding either that we had been touched by the sun or that we were looking at a movie set.

What is true of the practical world applies also to representational art. There is the same gradation of evidence from acquaintance to the use of increasingly extraneous signs, e.g., from the intimacy of genuine portraiture to the characterization of a person—usually a saint—by means of detached and separate attributes. And just as cognition in the outer world is unfit, once it abandons the physiognomic approach, to discover any but members of a logical class, so the use of diacritical marks in art prepares the establishment of a visual and iconographic type. Instead of recognizing St. Peter by the features of his face, of which all direct record has long been lost, we will then note his curly hair and beard, details that may have been distilled out of reminiscences of his appearance in the flesh. If even these are not sufficiently clear, although they are now stereotyped vouchers of identity, there remains, as a last clue to recognition, an outward diacritical sign, in this case the Key of Heaven which he holds in his hand.

It may also happen, because of this variety of cognitive tools, that the attributes and the physiognomy of a likeness are at odds, with the former pointing to a figure of the past while the latter renders a contemporary face. We then speak of mythological portraits, and imply that the rendition of the living person is dominant, relegating the incidental details to the status of attributes or, at best, of a sophisticated fancy dress. Whether it is the emperor Commodus who preens himself as Hercules with his lion skin, or an eighteenth-century lady who poses as Diana in pretty rococo costume, the outcome is always that the sitter is portrayed "in the role of" whomever he chooses to impersonate, the unity of representation being preserved by this gradation of histrionic evidence. On the other hand, when Florentine painters of the Renaissance give to the main actors in a sacred event the features of persons prominent in contemporary life, then the emphasis is reversed, for the total scene now prevails over subordinate physiognomic fact. It is now the Virgin Mary or the three Magi whom we see portrayed in the likenesses of individuals foreign to them. The unitary character of representation is saved by the fusion of two component referents.

Once we are confronted with the individual work of art, the further problem is bound to arise as to how we may distinguish its valid diagnostic signs from features without critical relevance. Not all characteristics which recommend themselves as such can be treated as diagnostic signs, since their validity depends on the conventions employed; and since these conventions are, in turn, the tribute the artist has paid to the demands of his historical environment, we find that cognitive marks in art are no less in need of confirmation from circumstance than their equivalents in the practical world. The historian, if he is to avoid errors of mistaken identity, must learn about the traditions on which the artist has relied, and then derive the choice of signs in a work of art from the peculiarities of its intellectual habitat.

There are two ways in which the pressure of convention is felt in art, first in the recognition of motifs that depend upon the stylistic customs in force, and then, once more, on a logically more elevated plane, in the knowledge of iconographic identities. It will not do, for instance, to believe that the depiction of animals with five or six legs in Assyrian sculpture points to a creature with an abnormal number of limbs. For an analysis of the conventions of ancient Near Eastern reliefs will show that the sculptor attacked each side of the block as if the other side did not exist, and merely rounded off the corners as a concession to the need for a unified shape. It was merely a consequence of this fundamental approach and not an attempt to render a freak when he gave to each exposed side its full complement of legs. Similarly, when we find in Medieval art that an object is located in the sky, aloof from all contact with the terrestrial world, this need not mean that the object is represented as floating in the air, since the conventions of the time took little account of natural laws. In contrast, during the Renaissance, when the reign of nature had been reaffirmed, the same placement of a figure would designate it as a celestial phenomenon.

The same caution must be observed in determining iconographic identities; visual prominence is not always a sign of diacritical relevancy. Contemporary costumes in fifteenth-century religious art are not meant to acquaint us with the period in which the sacred events took place, they merely satisfy a popular demand for closeness and actuality; whereas the same garments, if we see them in a picture by Meissonier, will be calculated to bring a period to life through the meticulous presentation of the correct *milieu*. Even if tradition fails to provide a hint as to the location of iconographic clues, the missing evidence can often be found within the picture itself. The rising sun in the "Nativity" by Robert Campin could be dismissed as a precociously realistic device were it not that one of the figures in the foreground holds a burning candle in his hand. The simultaneous presence of both the natural and the artificial light suggests an intention on the artist's part to present us with a symbolic reference to Christ as the rising sun and His victory over the weaker illumination of the Old Testament. Even the historical situation within which a picture was produced, may help to authenticate its diagnostic signs, provided it is possible to unearth a contemporary reference. The same can be said, with very little change, of its topographic site, of the place it holds within an architectural setting, or of its position within a cycle of other works of art. There is, in short, a very considerable range of traditions and situations which can be made to converge toward our understanding of identifying signs. Only if no such context can be found to enlighten us about our task are we compelled to draw in our nets and be content with a catch of generic sensory types.

It must finally be said that the derivation of cognitive signs from units of expressive form has had its profound influence upon the character and development of art. Such units are not likely to be discerned unless their recognition is easy and instantaneous. Since therefore the exceptional and the unknown are both beyond their usual scope, we find that the entities of which they are composed are also likely to be familiar to us or, if not, to be either close relatives or composites of familiar things. Every unknown entity in the representational arts must be read in terms of known ones, of which it embodies the signs; and it is thus easy to understand why in the entire history of art there have been so very few attempts to pass beyond the immediate sensory world toward the radically new and untried. All our efforts have been confined to the limits of our normal environment. Our prison is so strongly barred that not even the artist's most transcendant task, the delineation of the heavenly world and of the beings inhabiting it, has brought out anything on his part but the statement, suitably enhanced, of human forms and of others from our daily experience. When attempts are made to describe a subjectively fantastic world, as in the art of Jerome Bosch and of medieval *drôlerie*, all that occurs is a disintegration of familiar forms and their resetting in various extravagant ways.

Conversely, if we are to represent an entity possessing no familiar diacritical marks, then the task of assuring recognition is transferred to external agencies. It may then be necessary to resort to the use of titles and inscriptions, which will provide what the likeness itself cannot. It is possible, by virtue of such linguistic support, to extend the scope of direct representation far beyond anything that man has ever been able to see. The beholder may thus be convinced by the text that what, at first, seemed merely a complex concentric shape, more like an ornament than anything else, must be read as the illustration of a physical fact, in this case of the pattern of X-ray diffraction within a molecule. We also invoke the help of inscriptions when marks of cognition yield only a generic type, while we feel obliged to penetrate toward knowledge of a closer—perhaps even an individual—identity, e.g., when we learn what species of animal is portrayed from a glance at the caption of an illustrative plate.

The reader will have noticed, if he is critically inclined, that we have at times passed beyond the consideration of cognitive signs toward a discussion of immanent traits: features which should be kept apart, since one is an entity put to human use, while the other stays aloof on the phenomenal plain. It would be a mistake, we believe, to follow too closely the empiricist lead and to proclaim that "to be," in art, is "to be perceived." It is very natural, on the other hand, that this identity should have been assumed, for it is the fate of all diagnostic signs to be embodied and thus to become part of the representation which they help to explain. What at first had existed only in relation to us will then have turned into a self-sufficient detail capable of lending its aid, together with other auxiliary traits, toward the molding of a representational identity. As this process of merging proceeds, there will be a lowering of barriers around the diacritical mark, opening it to an intensified visual intercourse with other areas. The final result will be the setting up of an entity that will possess certain subordinate diacritical traits instead of being the victim of a semantic assault conducted through their agency. The siege machines will have turned into bulwarks of identity; and St. Peter, instead of waving his curly hair and beard at anyone eager to recognize him, will now guard them as intrinsic and constituent parts of his artistic personality. We shall be able to gauge the extent of this change of co-ordinates when we realize that even external signs, usually dismissed and forgotten as soon as their contribution is made, attain a permanent position in art. We refer to them under the name of attributes and we believe that their presence, e.g., of St. Catherine's wheel or of the lion purring at St. Jerome's feet, is essential for the completeness of a representational type. Their habitat is in that outer twilight of personality where property, in the logical acceptance of the term, merges with possession in its worldly and economic sense.

Thus a likeness must discharge the complex and multiple job of showing that representation is taking place, what it is that is being represented, and by virtue of what qualities the likeness discharges its task— a profusion of functions, the like of which no other form of representation is called upon to perform. The ambassador or lawyer will declare himself by handing in his credentials in advance or explaining what mission brought him into the presence of the interpretant, and samples and specimens are absolved from justifying their task, since it was staked out for them by the interpretant himself. The announcement of representation is here clearly distinct from its functioning; likenesses, by contrast, so concentrate their function in one single complex act that we cannot even know whether or not they are representational unless we have made a previous surmise as to the artist's intention. It is equally characteristic of them and of their mode of operation that as soon as we have begun to single out the marks of cognition which we need to find our way, these same marks are magically transformed and now burst upon our view as integrated parts of the entities they connote, all sense of intention having fallen by the wayside.

The process is usually a rapid one, prompted by a lifetime of experience in identifying visual facts. We should therefore be grateful that there exists one category of likenesses so contrived that the process is slowed down and its successive stages can be readily discerned. The trick images popular not so long ago present themselves at first as mere jumbles of lines, with the challenge that, as a kind of game, we discover their latent representational charge. Integration proceeds slowly by identifiable steps as some sector congeals into representational shape, then acts as a clue for unravelling other parts, which in turn activate areas elsewhere, until some measure of organization has spread throughout a previously chaotic design. Each time there is the same succession of events, beginning with the perception of a physiognomic Gestalt, passing from there to its hardening into a diacritical sign, and ending, as its task is duly discharged, with its merging into the established order of things.

Thus the description of recognition under a handicap compels us to introduce one more basic term, that of a minimum unit of perceptual significance, which we regard as the active principle in the recognition of representational form. Such units are the first to be grasped in the course of a perceptual act, because they are either so pregnant with physiognomic weight or so close to our previous experience of visual fact that recognition will be easy and instantaneous. Once their identity is established beyond a doubt, then their organizing influence will come into play, acting inward toward the interpretation of minor detail, and outward to compel other areas into loyalty toward a common significance. Wherever their constructive strength is felt, isolation and incongruity of form give way to concerted action in the visual field, and representation will expand. Even when they are turned into cognitive signs, their organizing function will be unimpaired, for such signs have their own blurred environment, whose indeterminacy they sharpen into actuality, so that there will be a functional harmony between structural and semantic agencies.

The nature of minimum physiognomic units will come home to us as we ask ourselves how much of our environment we must perceive at any one time in order to grasp the identity of objects contained in it. We may define them as entities just large enough to escape dissolution into the nondescript, but not so large that they will fall apart into accumulations of smaller entities. Thus if we contract our visual field we will reach the stage when we will have to forego immediate recognition of some familiar forms. Experience will show, on the other hand, that objects and physiognomic units do not coincide, and that recognition of the former may depend upon the place they hold within a familiar environment.

At least two characteristics will be found in such units of perceptual significance. The first is a constructive rule, an invariant almost independent of point of view, which decrees the position of subsidiary parts, the connections, and the range of proportion that may exist between them; the difference between the objects in our environment, e.g., a house, a chair, or a tree, being predicated upon the presence of such morphological singularities. The other characteristic assures our awareness of these singularities. It consists of the preponderance of outline over inner areas and helps to mold our sense impression into shapes and palpable configurations. If perception contained no such edges and boundaries, it would face a medley of murky surfaces, an assembly so amorphous and undifferentiated that there could be little awareness of clear-cut entities. Instead of those direct perceptions which enable us to orient ourselves we would have to rely upon tactile evidence in ascertaining identities. We will thus be hardly challenged when we claim that the reign of the contour, which is universal in the early phases of art, has its roots in the nature of perception itself.

But we cannot rest content with this statement, for it is characteristic of mimetic representation that it is never entirely determined by the visual materials that enter into the making of it. The mere fact that it is a projection upon a surface or upon a block of stone or of marble, which may be achieved by a variety of techniques, changes the nature of what is offered to us. There is thus a difference between an outline that is the boundary of an object, an exponent of its bulk and three-dimensional shape, and its creative use in the hands of the draftsman, whose work may at times seem to reverse the natural relation between object and visual edge. If we are to understand this phenomenon, we must supplement the analysis of perception and of artificial configurations by another glance at the theory of representation itself.

The reader will remember that earlier in this book, before the subject of likeness came into view, we stated that representation, in all of its forms, acts only by virtue of certain chosen traits, without implicating the totality at stake, since, in representation, being and function do not coincide; and we made the further claim that the areas omitted are mobilized by the influence of the active areas, instead of remaining inert and indifferent. We showed that a lawyer is a representative, although not all of his words and surely not all of his personality are at the direct service of his task as a delegate; and that specimens operate because of circumscribed traits which happen to attract the interest of the interpretant. We have now come to the corresponding phenomenon in the working of images and likenesses, where there is a similar dichotomy between leading traits and dependent areas. And just as we accord to a delegate his dignity as a representative because his words affirm the assumption of appointment and common interest, so we find that in likenesses a few strokes of the pen suffice to create the illusion of resemblance and of material embodiment. Some lines, judiciously placed by a master's hand, will pull the white paper into their sphere, loading its untrodden emptiness with representational significance. And so strong is the interconnection of such areas with their activating agencies that these lines will immediately lose their physiognomic significance if we perform the mental act of separating them from their nondescript environment. It is necessary, on the other hand, to find a compromise between artistic means and physiognomic fact, if the drawing is to be representational, and to discover how its pregnant parts—those which we called minimum units of perception—can be made to radiate to and thereby to organize the areas of lesser cognitive charge. Thus in the course of the individuation of a subject the artist may stop at any intermediate stage, provided he has found a place within its array of forms for the necessary cognitive marks. He may produce a work of art that will be preliminary, yet complete, capable of being enjoyed, although compelled to forego much of its future embellishment and detail.

There exists, however, another type of art, for which this allusion is the final form, since this art is content to delineate diagnostic signs and to interpret them as if their combination were sufficient to stand for the total appearance of things. What we call archaic art is based on the simple notion that, in order to represent objects, one need only show the traits by which they are conventionally and publicly known. And since the task of ensuring that recognition occurs is antecedent to every other artistic ambition, it has been tempting to stop at this preliminary stage, to consolidate it through the adoption of a representational style, and to resist all further change. To surmount this barrier has been notoriously difficult, and it is one of the glories of ancient Greek art that it was the first to succeed in liberating itself from archaic restraints. We shall define archaic art as a practice that looks upon the thing portrayed as an aggregate of embodied diagnostic marks instead of regarding it as a living thing maintained by the interaction of its inner energies. As a consequence of this fundamental attitude the life of the image is limited to its surface, which is not yet conceived as the

outer boundary of the forces contained by it. In archaic
art all those parts that could function as diagnostic
signs are portrayed from their most easily recognizable
aspects; nor does the archaic artist hesitate to pull
nature apart if he can thus obtain a convincing collection of significant traits. He may thus, as in Egyptiav
art, render the human eye from the front but the face
from the side, the trunk of the body again from the
front, and the arms and legs once more in the profile
view—all this, paradoxically, in the name of completeness and intelligibility. Since units of cognition are
circumscribed—their gist residing in their well-marked
outline—large areas remain unclaimed, and the material
may shine through them unless their emptiness is canceled out by space-filling ornament. Hence the obedience
of painting to the picture plane, and the bare inert
heaviness of sculpture in early art. Hence also the tendency among those who are disturbed by such vacant
areas to dissolve the image into ornament by singling
out its constituent parts, exaggerating, transposing,
and interlacing them until little of the original surface
remains. This is the case of the earliest Chinese art, and
also of Mayan and early Germanic art.

To the archaic artist the distance from which a
thing is viewed, the aspect under which it appears, and
the perspective distortions of its shape are all equally
irrelevant, for they are all due to the object's fortuitous
relation to an interpretant and thus detract from its
invariant qualities. Nor can he pay attention to the
phenomena of light and atmosphere, which are the tokens
of an interaction of the object with an environment,
for these too must appear to him as ephemeral circumstances unworthy of his interest. The kind of likeness
which arises out of considerations such as these—all

of them usually unconscious and so compulsive that the artist does not know of the existence of alternatives— is well known to anybody acquainted with the art of children and of the ancient Orient. It shows its object as an isolated entity, well-defined by its outline, composed of equally distinct component parts, colored in the hues which the mind attributes to its kind, oriented frontally, and without any but the essential details—an image without mood or implied profundity, stated but not really understood, its greatest merit the sensitivity and simplicity of its outline, which the paucity of details has rendered possible.

An artist who operates with embodied diagnostic marks is not apt to rise to the portrayal of individual things, for an approach that emphasizes the single factor at the expense of a larger physiognomic whole is alien to him. He may produce an image of a tree complete with all that pertains to its generic life, but not of this particular tree, which happens to stand at the corner of the neighboring park; and when he draws a human face, he may provide it with all that goes into the making of it, including perhaps some signs of race or some attributes of social estate, but the intimacies of a portrait will be foreign to him. It is only when the figure is meant to substitute for an individual man conceived in all his uniqueness that archaic art may surpass itself, as it did in Egypt, and proceed to the successful rendition of portrait qualities.

The way out of the archaic impasse is marked by the very nature of the restrictions it imposes upon art. We claimed that archaic art is an assembly of diagnostic marks, and that it activates only those minimum aspects, usually concentrated in the outline, that are required for the recognition of the entities portrayed.

The emancipation from archaism consists of the gradual activation of intervening parts, with surfaces turning into boundaries of living things and the previous definitory use of lines giving way either to their dissolution into light and shade or their conception as ridges between independent planes. Thus all that had been a play with selected features on the surface of things is now replaced by the conception of exterior planes as exponents of living forces within. And since the entire surface has now acquired an ability to respond to forces that remain unseen, the way is prepared for the further step of opening it to influences from the outer world. A gradual evolution will thus yield the discovery of the perspective point of view, as well as of the effects of light and atmosphere.

The area around the likeness will be similarly transformed. Originally a neutral background or rather the foil before which all concrete action unfolds, and thus representational only in an indirect and supplementary sense, it will begin to fill up with landscape and architectural shapes. The complete activation of the background will be attained when its emptiness is entirely cancelled out, and when the former plane of parchment or wall surface will have turned into the colored expanse of the sky. The shift in the role of subordinate parts could not be better attested than by this change from something that is latent and unproclaimed to an explicit representation of visual fact.

We shall end by observing that any natural shape that is large enough for its perceptual meaning to be grasped, can also function as a visual entity in art. It is this consideration of minimum size which determines how much of an object may disappear behind another, overlapping one without causing a total loss of intelligibility. And while there is a very natural preference for such total configurations as "a house," "a man," or "a tree," it is always possible to dissolve them into parts, provided that what remains is still an entity in its fragmentary state. Only when we encounter small independent parts which we are not accustomed to see alone unless they appear in an ornamental array, such as a hand, an eye, or a leaf, will there be such a loss of context that they will either stand before us clamoring for the connotations of which they are deprived or find their bearings in a universe of subjective experience.

Whether such an entity will be able to stand for the totality of which it is part will depend upon its rank on the physiognomic scale and secondarily also upon its environment. We all accept the conventions of portraiture, which render a person by the features of his face, merely adding, in order to stabilize the design, his neck and the anatomical regions adjoining it. For the face is so dominant in our experience of man, so pregnant with character and with the history of his life that it will suffice in itself to evoke him in his totality. It would not occur to us to regard such a portrait as truncated and incomplete. But if we were to represent only the area downward from the lower margin of the bust we should find the implicit totality replaced by the painful sensation of a human body cut in two.

Where the physiognomic charge is insufficient to enforce acceptance of a part for the whole, the justification for such acceptance may come from the environment. Just as in language the synecdoche will blossom forth if its meaning is made clear by the framework of a phrase, so the abbreviated visual image must receive its charge from the context in which it appears. A tree will represent a forest, a soldier the military forces of which he is part, only if the surrounding likeness demands this mental progress from the single to the comprehensive fact. What context can do for a *pars pro toto* can be seen from the extreme case of a political caricature that designated a dictator of recent notoriety merely by the ominous little mustache, enough at the time to evoke his unsavory personality. Today, only two decades later, the allusion already seems too concentrated to be understood.

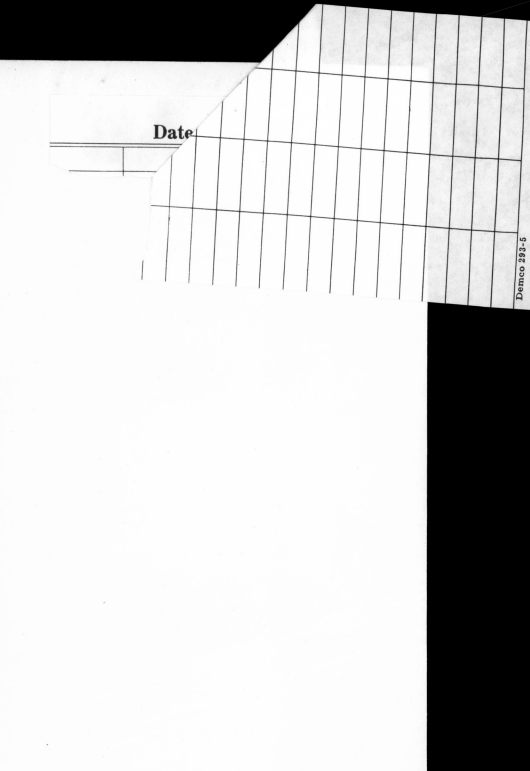

Date

Demco 293-5